IMAGES
*of America*

# J.N. "DING" DARLING
# NATIONAL WILDLIFE REFUGE

The Sanibel Island Light Station, pictured above in 1949, became operational in August 1884. After damage by major hurricanes in 1944 and 1947, the quarters were determined unsafe for US Coast Guard personnel and their dependents. The agency automated the light and left Sanibel Island. The US Fish and Wildlife Service signed a revocable permit on June 21, 1949, and leased the property from the Coast Guard. The light station served as headquarters for the Sanibel (later, J.N. "Ding" Darling) National Wildlife Refuge for the next 33 years. (Sanibel Historical Museum and Village.)

ON THE COVER: The cover photograph records a battery of serious bird photographers lined up along the refuge's Wildlife Drive in 1990. With the advantage of telephoto lenses, they have approached as close as they can physically position themselves to hundreds of foraging colonial birds. Egrets, herons, and ibises, even brown pelicans, have congregated on the shallow flats across the deep borrow canal, in a refuge impoundment. These water birds put on a spectacular show when water levels drop and their aquatic prey consolidates in shallow pockets of water. The hungry birds crowd together in an amazing, energetic feeding frenzy. (US Fish and Wildlife Service.)

IMAGES
*of America*

# J.N. "DING" DARLING
# NATIONAL WILDLIFE REFUGE

Charles LeBuff

ARCADIA
PUBLISHING

Published by Arcadia Publishing
Charleston, South Carolina


Library of Congress Control Number: 2010943012

For all general information, please contact Arcadia Publishing:
Telephone 843-853-2070
Fax 843-853-0044
E-mail sales@arcadiapublishing.com
For customer service and orders:
Toll-Free 1-888-313-2665

Visit us on the Internet at www.arcadiapublishing.com

*In memory of W.D. "Tommy" Wood, my friend and mentor—
and the best "boss" a wildlife refuge worker could ever hope for.*

# CONTENTS

# ACKNOWLEDGMENTS

Without the understanding and support of my wife, Jean, this book would never have gotten off the launch pad. Lise Bryant, bookstore manager for the "Ding" Darling Wildlife Society, suggested that I tackle this project and helped in many ways. Paul Tritaik, refuge manager at J.N. "Ding" Darling National Wildlife Refuge (NWR), provided access to the refuge's Annual Narrative Reports and photograph files, and took the time to review the final manuscript. Retired refuge managers John Eadie, Denny Holland, and Bill Julian were very helpful. Denny is the son of Ernie Holland, an old-school refuge manager who often visited Sanibel to vacation with his wife, Eileen, in the exclusive "Sanibel Refuge Motel." Mark Madison, US Fish and Wildlife Service historian, kindly made several images available. Additionally, many photographs were obtained from other official sources of the Service. Captions for these images are credited as USFWS. Sanibel historian Betty Anholt graciously reviewed the final manuscript. Francis Bailey, patriarch of the Sanibel family that has supported the refuge from its beginning, gave valuable input and provided photographs. The following islanders and friends of J.N. "Ding" Darling NWR were extremely helpful: Ralph Woodring and Jim Pickens, both of whom I once shared a Fort Myers High School English class with; Virginia Stokes Merritt and her nephew Marty Stokes; Andrea and "Kip" Koss ("Ding" Darling's grandson); Kristie Anders, once the author's coworker at the refuge; longtime island newspaperwoman Anne Bellew; and Jim Fowler, publisher of the exquisite Sanibel-Captiva Nature Calendar. Don Claytor and Roger Zocki, both retirees of the Lee County Mosquito Control District, came to the rescue and helped with a great photograph and a refreshing overview of the district's Sanibel operations. Former Sanibelian Paul Zajicek provided invaluable archival support in Tallahassee. Last, but not least, Arcadia Publishing's Lindsay Harris Carter was a gem of an editor to work with.

# INTRODUCTION

I have a unique intimacy with the history of J.N. "Ding" Darling National Wildlife Refuge. It is a personal connection unlike any connection with a living person. As a young man, near the beginning of my 32-year career with the US Fish and Wildlife Service, at what then was known as the Sanibel NWR, I shared some awesome and memorable hours with an articulate, loud-voiced, complex old man named Jay Norwood "Ding" Darling. Our conversation over those two days in December 1959 shaped my life and firmly entrenched me in the conservation ethic of Sanibel Island, my new home. His most memorable words to me on the first day we met, sharing coffee with his friend, refuge manager Tommy Wood, became a challenge to conserve sea turtles: "Those little turtles don't have a . . . chance in hell of making it . . . it's critical that you do everything you can to help and protect them. Someone just has to!" I took his words seriously and for the next 32 years, some of my official time and most of my free time was devoted to that cause.

Tommy had told me about how a few years earlier, and with money out of his own pocket, Mr. Darling had purchased an acre of Sanibel Slough property from Frank P. Bailey before the Fish and Wildlife Service closed on the purchase of the 100-acre parcel that would become known as the Bailey Tract. In addition, he paid for the cost of drilling a four-inch artesian well on that one-acre parcel. This flowing well continuously discharged 9,000 gallons of water per hour into the adjacent wetlands. It formed, even at the driest part of the year, a small pool of water in the Bailey Tract's wetland system that would otherwise seasonally dry up until the barren bottom actually cracked wide open. Fissures in the mud and shell nearly two feet deep opened during the worst droughts. Without much ado, Darling personally financed the first attempt to insure that permanent, year-round fresh surface water was available in the wetlands to sustain Sanibel's fish and wildlife resources. The second try, using dynamite, followed a few days later.

By the time I met him, Mr. Darling had sold his Captiva Island properties, and he and his wife would spend their remaining winters near their son in Clearwater, Florida, until they could no longer make the arduous trip from Iowa. It was only because the Darlings made the effort and drove down to Captiva for a few days to enjoy a final visit with their old friends that our paths crossed. I was in the right place at the right time.

I also learned during that morning's discussion that "Ding" Darling was genuinely concerned for the region's marine resources. He gave the University of Miami's Marine Laboratory a donation to help fund a preliminary investigation into the red tides that periodically impacted the Southwest Florida coast. He had seen this devastation personally in the waters around Sanibel and Captiva, first in 1946. These sporadic events seemingly killed almost every aquatic organism living in the inshore waters of the Gulf of Mexico. It surprised me to learn that even at his advanced age, Mr. Darling continued to make personal demands on and criticize the people he still knew in high levels of government. He was insistent that something had to be done to understand this phenomenon. The impacts on tourism and the local fisheries concerned him greatly. His constant pressure via a flurry of personal letters helped get the US Fish and Wildlife Service involved, and in 1956, the Service's Bureau of Commercial Fisheries staffed a red tide field station, an equipped marine laboratory, down the coast in Naples. Coincidentally, I had started my federal career at this laboratory, and this is where I met Tommy Wood. I flew with Tommy in the government-owned Piper Tri-Pacer seaplane that was used part-time for the needs of the laboratory. We made weekly water sample collecting trips together between Pass-a-Grille, near Tampa Bay, and Marathon, in the Florida Keys. When it was time to add a second permanent position to Sanibel NWR, Tommy Wood selected me.

When the opportunity to write this book presented itself, I was excited. Nearly 50 years of my life is inextricably connected to "Ding" Darling's wildlife refuge, and the community in which it is located. Throughout development of this work, I strived to create a book that is more than a personal photo album. This has been a most difficult course to steer, because I have, at this writing, been part of the refuge for half of its existence.

—Charles LeBuff

# One

# SANYBEL ISLAND

Sanibel Island is a crescent-shaped barrier island on the Southwest Florida coast. Located in Lee County, it is three miles from the mouth of the Caloosahatchee, a 70-mile-long river that connects Lake Okeechobee with the Gulf of Mexico. Originally named Puerto Sur Nivel by the Spanish, the island's name linguistically corrupted to Sanybel by the 18th century. English-speaking settlers moved down the peninsula and displaced the Spanish by the middle of the 19th century. In 1888, after land on Sanybel Island became available, as provided by the 1862 Homestead Act, homesteaders arrived on Sanybel Island and its place name evolved into Sanibel Island. The US Post Office shortened the island's name to Sanibel by 1895 in an act of brevity for postmark purposes. After islanders incorporated as a city in 1974, the new city council officially changed the island's name to Sanibel.

Unlike most barrier islands along Florida's coastline, which are aligned north and south, Sanibel has a curved east-to-west alignment. Shallow waters surround its perimeter and are coupled with an important estuary and mangrove forest on the island's northern periphery. These submerged bottoms provide habitat for more than 400 species of seashells. The abundance of collectable shells on the island's 12-mile-long Gulf beach has attracted people for over a century. Sanibel's center is basin-like and of varying elevation. Longitudinally, the island's interior landscape is composed of shell ridges and low depressions, called swales, which were created by powerful prehistoric hurricanes. The widest of these swales is known as the Sanibel Slough, which, at its broadest point, is one mile across and dominated by cord grass. The long upland ridges are vegetated with cabbage palms and an understory of tropical West Indian hardwoods. The Sanibel Slough floods each summer and attracts extremely large populations of colonial nesting birds and migratory waterfowl. This is why early conservationists, like "Ding" Darling, wanted to see these wetland systems publicly acquired and protected. The downside to the alternating cycles of flooding and drying out is the overwhelming population of nuisance salt marsh mosquitoes that bred in the Sanibel Slough.

This 1562 map was created 49 years after Juan Ponce de León "discovered" Florida. Most historians who study this period believe that the Castilian conquistador sailed into what is now San Carlos Bay, next to Sanibel, in May 1513. The expedition was soon assaulted by a large force of Calusa Indians, warlike Native Americans, who would continue to fiercely resist the repeated Spanish attempts to colonize Calusa territory in Southwest Florida for several generations after Juan Ponce de León's arrival. This map is a fine example of the period's cartography. (Department of College Archives and Special Collections, Olin Library, Rollins College, Winter Park, Florida.)

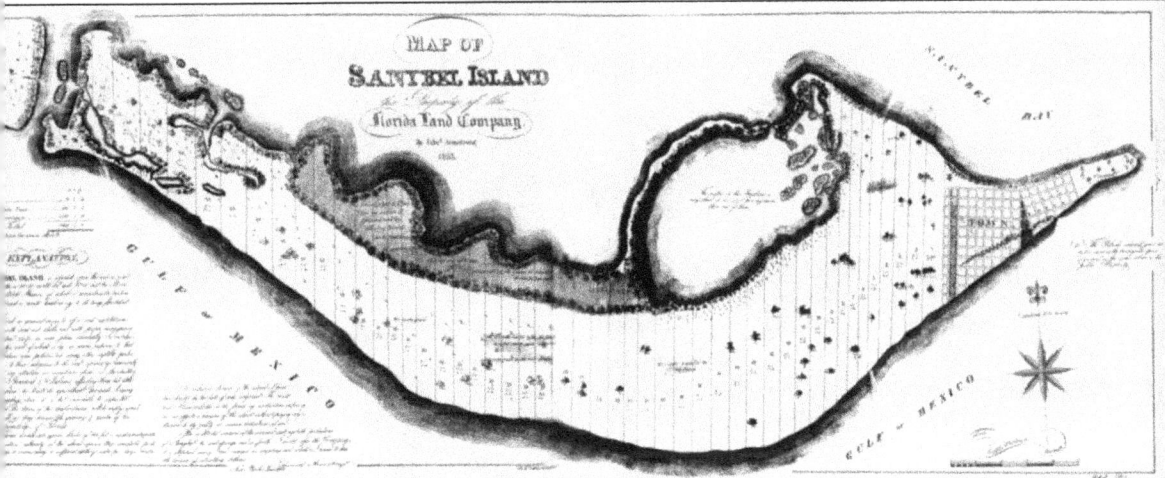

In the early 1830s, a group of northern real estate investors acquired a questionable title to Sanybel Island. It was included in a huge Spanish land grant that spread across most of south-central Florida. The financiers formed the Florida Land Company. By 1833, their plans for development were published in the form of the above plat map. Settlers began to purchase parcels, but most were discouraged from physically working the land because of the frequency of hurricanes, mosquito density, and the Second Seminole War (1835–1842). The Spanish land grants were later invalidated by American courts. Sanybel Island was determined to be federal public domain land by the time Florida became the 27th state in 1845. In 1850, most of the island became eligible to be transferred to state ownership when Congress passed a new version of the Swamp and Overflow Land Act to include Florida. It would not be until 1884 that the first permanent residents arrived on Sanibel, employees of the US Lighthouse Establishment. (Betty Anholt and Sanibel Historical Museum and Village.)

This 1936 postcard illustrates the wildness of Sanibel. Periwinkle Way is visible in the center and to its left are the savannahs of the Sanibel Slough. These wetlands along with the shallows of the tidal estuary have historically attracted great numbers of birds. The lighthouse compound at Point Ybel is to the lower right, and the bend that is just out of the photograph at the left margin is Knapp's Point. (Francis Bailey.)

This photograph was taken in 1955, prior to mosquito control operations in the Sanibel Slough. The breakout point of the rainfall-swollen slough is visible on the Gulf beach. It is the triangular indentation of beach to the left of the most distant foreground buildings and the neighborhood grid of side streets. (James Pickens.)

Pictured here, the Sanibel Slough's breakout was 0.8 miles west of the lighthouse on the Gulf beach. When the basin filled to capacity, its dark water flowed through this breach and became the Sanibel River. In 1949, the refuge manager planned with other organizations to block this outfall with a water-control structure. Effective water management in the slough could not be attained if all the water was allowed to drain away. (James Pickens.)

The upper photograph, from 1960, shows the Mosquito Control District's water control structure in the lower center. This is the island's major dam that ties the Slough to Tarpon Bay. This structure had removable flashboards to prevent flooding before the Sanibel River got high enough to break through the beach to drain the Slough basin. The diagonal road in the upper left of the lower photograph is Bailey Road, and the lower left diagonal road is Beach Road. The modern Beach Road Weir is just out of this photograph. The river's original course remains relatively untouched in this 1960 photograph, but its alteration is looming; one major subdivision called Sanibel Estates is completed and Shell Harbor is conceived. (Above, USFWS; below, US Natural Resources Conservation Service.)

Between 1928 and 1963, the islands were accessible on a daylight-only schedule via the Kinzie Brothers Steamer Line. In this photograph, their ferryboat the *Rebel* is headed for Punta Rassa. This vessel carried nine automobiles at a one-way cost of a dollar for the car, and 50¢ each for the driver and passengers. When the Kinzie ferry service ended, four ferries were in service during the winter's peak tourist season. (James Pickens.)

The Sanibel Ferry Landing is shown in 1963. In the distance are the new Sanibel Causeway and its raised bascule bridge. A sign at the ferry landing welcomed visitors to Sanibel National Wildlife Refuge. All lands within the boundary of the 1947 Presidential Closure Order were considered refuge, and calculations for all manner of wildlife surveys and public-use records were considered on-refuge. (James Pickens.)

Pictured above is the Sanibel Causeway at completion. Notwithstanding opposition against this bridge by island residents and support for their position from the US Fish and Wildlife Service, the Lee County Board of County Commissioners turned a deaf ear. Fish and Wildlife Service biologists outlined the deleterious effects the two proposed spoil islands would have on salinities in the estuary. Lee County officials were determined to see the islands accessible and developed. The photograph below looks across the causeway from Sanibel. The impacts that Fish and Wildlife Service biologists forecasted came to pass. Since the causeway was completed, water quality has suffered, and valuable marine resources have dwindled. The causeway opened on May 26, 1963, and the islands and refuge began to change. (Above, L.L. Cook Company; below, O'Brien Color Studios.)

When the Service adopted national sign standards, all entrance signs in the South Florida Refuges Complex were replaced with routed redwood signs (above). They were stained dark brown, and the blue goose and lettering was yellow. The two signs pictured were located near the end of the causeway in 1969. They informed visitors when they were entering or leaving the refuge. Below, the sign's design utilizes local quahog clams, in keeping with a Sanibel theme. (Both, USFWS.)

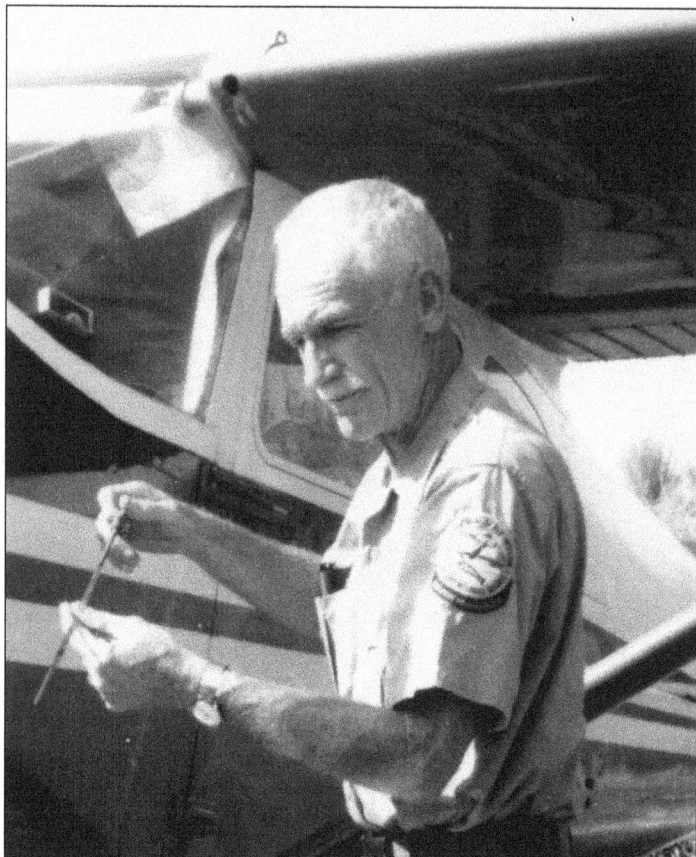

In 1958, refuge manager Tommy Wood (pictured at left, in 1969) hired Charles LeBuff (pictured below, also in 1969) as the second permanent refuge employee. Both men remained on Sanibel for the duration of their Service careers and retired from their refuge positions—Wood in 1971, and LeBuff in 1990. (Both, USFWS.)

## Two

# A Man Named "Ding" and the Birth of the Sanibel Refuge

Jay Norwood Darling was born in Norwood, Michigan, on October 21, 1876. By 1913, he was a popular editorial cartoonist, working for the *Des Moines Register and Leader* in Iowa, and was soon syndicated in 130 daily newspapers across America. Early on, Darling established a reputation as a personality concerned with national policies that, in his view, were destroying America's wetlands. In 1934, he was recruited by Pres. Franklin Roosevelt to head the US Bureau of Biological Survey, the predecessor of the US Fish and Wildlife Service. An outgrowth of this appointment later led to his election as the first president of the National Wildlife Federation. In 1935, "Ding" and his wife, Genevieve "Penny" Darling, discovered Captiva Island, then a secluded barrier island off the coast of Southwest Florida. Captiva was joined to its larger neighbor Sanibel by a one-lane wooden bridge spanning Blind Pass, but they were accessible from the mainland only by boat or seaplane. Both islands were perceived by Darling to be in the throes of a conservation crisis. Subsistence taking of protected wildlife was traditional among the 200 year-round residents of the islands. Real estate promoters were vigorously trying to purchase state-owned wild lands on the northern periphery of Sanibel Island. These lands and their tidal system were critically important for resident and migratory birds.

Sanibel Island is geologically unique among regional barrier islands. In cross-section, it is a broad wetland basin that is dammed, completely encircled, by ancient beach ridges. This basin regularly floods each summer and historically, when the contained water crested at its highest elevation, with nowhere else to go, it broke through the Gulf beach ridge to become a flowing river. When flooded, it was primary foraging habitat for resident and migratory birds. During annual dry cycles, it was the production center for Sanibel's notorious and dreaded mosquito population.

By 1936, "Ding" Darling joined residents of the islands and developed a grassroots approach they hoped would lead to the protection of the area's wildlife resources. They formed the Inter Island Conservation Association, and under Darling's inspirational leadership, the group forged ahead to meet their goals.

Jay Norwood "Ding" Darling (1876–1962) is pictured here. This extraordinary man took the helm and steered the difficult course through the winding channels of high-level bureaucracy to insure that, eventually, almost half of Sanibel would be saved as a national wildlife refuge. For nearly 25 years, he endeared himself to the people of Sanibel and Captiva Islands as he shared their passion for advocating the protection of these fragile islands. In the end, his friends memorialized him in a most fitting way. (Andrea and Kip Koss.)

This cartoon, published in 1936, was one of Darling's most meaningful. Students of his work suggest that he used Captiva and Sanibel Islands as a foundation on which to base his creative mind-set when developing this piece. It certainly is prophetic when the changes to the islands since are put into perspective. He aptly titled this cartoon, "The History of Utopia." Since then, others have named it, "The Outline of History." ("Ding" Darling Wildlife Society.)

J.N. "Ding" Darling's nickname evolved from his habit of abbreviating his surname into "D'ing" whenever he signed one of his cartoons. Over time, he eventually dropped the internal apostrophe. Darling found humor in this nickname and autographed his work with this unique freestyle contraction. He was soon known nationwide by this pen name. Pictured are both his pen name and a self-rendered caricature, hard at work at the drawing board. ("Ding" Darling Wildlife Society.)

In 1934, after being appointed to head the Bureau of Biological Survey, "Ding" Darling designed the first Migratory Bird Hunting Stamp, or the Duck Stamp. The purchase of this federal stamp allows the buyer to harvest migratory waterfowl. Monies from stamp sales are used exclusively to buy wetlands, and the purchase of millions of acres of habitat has since increased the size of the National Wildlife Refuge System. "Ding" Darling's design for the stamp's artwork is shown above. Below is the printed 1934–1935 Duck Stamp. New stamps were created in successive years, and today, this program hosts a highly competitive national art contest to select the next Duck Stamp. (Above, "Ding" Darling Wildlife Society; below, USFWS.)

A national Junior Duck Stamp competition was developed in the 1990s. The concept originated at the Sanibel Elementary School and was developed by art instructor Jaye Boswell. The first winning entry in the national contest was rendered by Jason Parsons, of Canton, Illinois, and is pictured above. In the photograph below, "Ding" Darling's grandson Christopher "Kip" Koss is judging entries in an early Junior Duck Stamp competition. (Both, USFWS.)

Darling's artistic repertoire went beyond creating thought-provoking, leading-edge political and conservation cartoons. As a personal hobby, he produced a series of waterfowl- and hunting-themed etchings. In a 1941 letter to fellow artist and renowned etcher Levon West, Darling wrote, "I am still a rotten etcher." Creating etchings is a difficult and painstaking art form, but Darling was a perfectionist at the craft. His were not rendered commercially, but were distributed as gifts to his friends. The above etching was titled *Explosion in the Lily Pads* and, at left, *After Closing Hour They All Come In.* (Both, "Ding" Darling Wildlife Society.)

Among the credits to Darling's creative art skills—and his long-lasting impacts on the Fish and Wildlife Service—was his design of the blue goose, in 1934–1935. His blue goose was first used on refuge signs in 1936, and has since become the traditional symbol of the National Wildlife Refuge System. The sign design pictured at right, from 1936, bears the first blue goose on the boundary sign, designed by Darling for the Bureau of Biological Survey. Every refuge boundary sign and most refuge entrance signs are identified with Darling's blue stylized goose. The sign below was used on the Sanibel Refuge in the late 1940s. These early blue goose signs were made from expensive porcelain-covered steel. Modern boundary signs are aluminum. (Right, USFWS; below, author.)

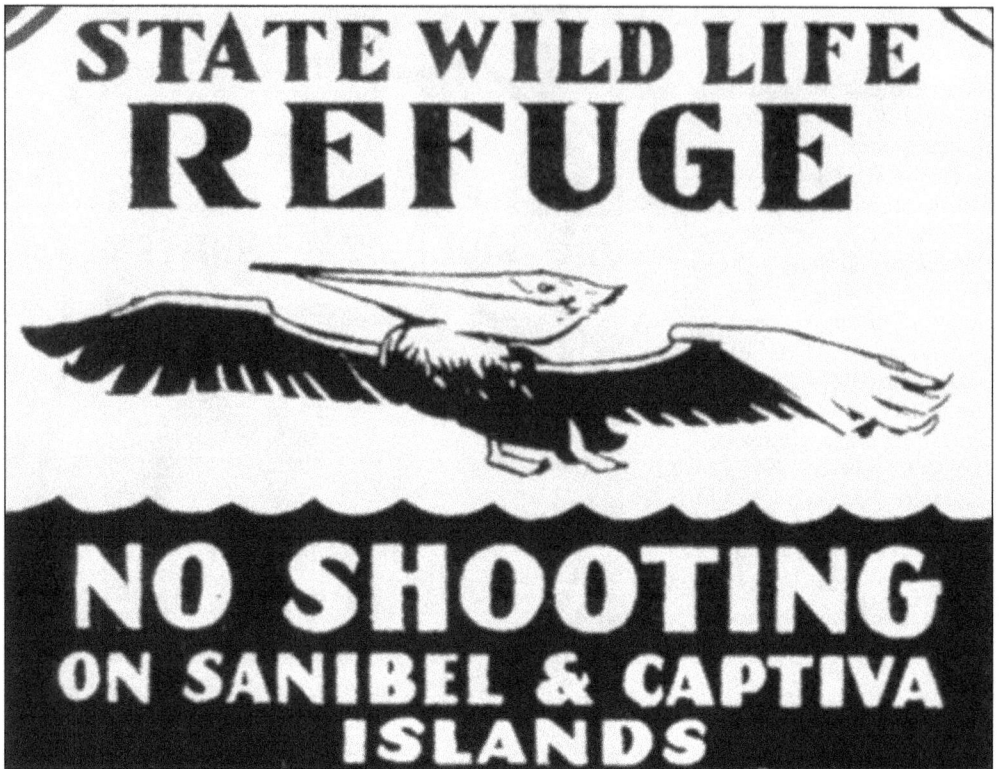

STATE WILD LIFE
REFUGE

NO SHOOTING
ON SANIBEL & CAPTIVA
ISLANDS

This pelican image bears witness to Darling's creativity. In 1939, the Florida State Legislature passed House Bill 1095. In part, it states, "An Act to Establish a Game and Fish Refuge in Certain Portions of Lee County and to Provide for Enforcement and Punishment for Violation Thereof; To Establish a Refuge Commission and Prescribe the Qualifications of Its Members." Section 1 of this act describes the refuge as, "the Islands of Sanibel and Captiva including all the land areas on said Islands." The Refuge Commission hired Muggins Underhill as a part-time warden in 1943. The commission was abolished in 1960 because a refuge manager was in place and the group obsolete. Those who served on the commission were Ernest Bailey, Francis Bailey Jr., Hallie Matthews, Della Mitchell, William D. Wood, and Webb Shanahan, of Sanibel. Captiva members included Belton Johnson, Max Hayford, and Allen Weeks. ("Ding" Darling Wildlife Society.)

FEDERAL REGISTER

VOLUME 12    1934    NUMBER 235,

Washington, Wednesday, December 3, 1947

TITLE 3—THE PRESIDENT

PROCLAMATION 2758

CLOSED AREA UNDER THE MIGRATORY BIRD TREATY ACT—FLORIDA

BY THE PRESIDENT OF THE UNITED STATES OF AMERICA

A PROCLAMATION

WHEREAS the Acting Secretary of the Interior has submitted to me for approval the following regulation adopted by him, after notice and public procedure pursuant to section 4 of the Administrative Procedure Act of June 11, 1946 (60 Stat. 238), under authority of the Migratory Bird Treaty Act of July 3, 1918 (40 Stat. 755, 16 U. S. C. 704), and Reorganization Plan No. II (53 Stat. 1431):

REGULATION DESIGNATING AS CLOSED AREA CERTAIN LANDS AND WATERS WITHIN, ADJACENT TO, OR IN THE VICINITY OF THE SANIBEL NATIONAL WILDLIFE REFUGE, FLORIDA

By virtue of and pursuant to the authority contained in section 3 of the Migratory Bird Treaty Act of July 3, 1918 (40 Stat. 755, 16 U. S. C. 704), Reorganization Plan No. II (53 Stat. 1431), and in accordance with the provisions of section 4 of the Administrative Procedure Act of June 11, 1946 (60 Stat. 238), I, Oscar L. Chapman, Acting Secretary of the Interior, having due regard to the zones of temperature and to the distribution, abundance, economic value, breeding habits, and times and lines of flight of the migratory birds included in the terms of the conventions between the United States and Great Britain for the protection of migratory birds, concluded August 16, 1916, and between the United States and the United Mexican States for the protection of migratory birds and game mammals, concluded February 7, 1936, do hereby designate as closed area, effective thirty days after publication in the FEDERAL REGISTER, in or on which pursuing, hunting, taking, capturing, or killing of migratory birds, or attempting to take, capture, or kill migratory birds is not permitted, all areas of land and water in Lee County, Florida, not now owned or controlled by the United States within the following-described exterior boundary:

Beginning at low water east of Sanibel Island Light, situated on Point Ybel on the east end of Sanibel Island, Florida, in approximate latitude 26°27'13" N., longitude 82°00'48" W.;

Thence Northwesterly with low water along the northeast side of Sanibel Island approximately 5170 yards (2.94 miles) to a point at low water and approximately 704 yards (0.40 mile) southeast of Woodrings Point on Sanibel Island;

Thence Northwesterly, within Pine Island Sound, approximately 1760 yards (1.00 mile) to St. James Light 3, in St. James City Channel, between Sanibel and Pine Islands;

Thence Northwesterly, Southwesterly and then Northwesterly continuing through Pine Island Sound by straight lines connecting in order the following navigation markers: St. James Daybeacon 7 (black); Pine Island Sound Daybeacon 8 (red); Pine Island Sound Light 10; Pine Island Sound Daybeacon 12 (red); Pine Island Sound Daybeacon 14 (red); Pine Island Sound Daybeacon 15 (black); Pine Island Sound Light 16, approximately 11,616 yards (6.60 miles) to Wulfert Daybeacon 1 (black), at the entrance to Wulfert Channel;

Thence Westerly and Southwesterly in Wulfert Channel and between Sanibel and Captiva Islands by straight lines connecting in order the following navigation markers: Wulfert Daybeacon 3 (black); Wulfert Daybeacon 5 (black); Wulfert Daybeacon 7 (black); Horn Passage Daybeacon 2 (red), approximately 3052 yards (1.74 miles) to Horn Passage Daybeacon 3 (black);

Thence Southerly approximately 628 yards (0.36 mile) to the center of the highway bridge connecting Sanibel and Captiva Islands;

Thence Westerly with the center of bridge and the prolongation thereof, across Captiva Island approximately 506 yards (0.29 mile) to low water on the west shore of Captiva Island;

Thence Westerly at right angles to the shore of Captiva Island, 440 yards (0.25 mile) to a point in the Gulf of Mexico;

Thence Southeasterly, Easterly and then Northeasterly, in the Gulf of Mexico, parallel to and 440 yards (0.25 mile) from low water along the south shore of Captiva and Sanibel Islands approximately 24,024 yards (13.65 miles) to a point in the Gulf of Mexico;

Thence Northwesterly 440 yards (0.25 mile) to the place of Beginning.

IN WITNESS WHEREOF, I have hereunto subscribed my name and caused the seal of the Department of the Interior to be affixed this tenth day of November 1947.

[SEAL]    OSCAR L. CHAPMAN,
Acting Secretary of the Interior.

(Continued on p. 8041)

AND WHEREAS upon consideration it appears that the foregoing regulation will tend to effectuate the purposes of the aforesaid Migratory Bird Treaty Act of July 3, 1918:

NOW, THEREFORE, I, HARRY S. TRUMAN, President of the United States of America, under and by virtue of the authority vested in me by the aforesaid Migratory Bird Treaty Act of July 3, 1918, do hereby approve and proclaim the foregoing regulation of the Acting Secretary of the Interior.

IN WITNESS WHEREOF I have hereunto set my hand and caused the Seal of the United States of America to be affixed.

DONE at the City of Washington this 2nd day of December in the year of our Lord nineteen hundred and [SEAL] forty-seven, and of the Independence of the United States of America the one hundred and seventy-second.

HARRY S. TRUMAN

By the President:
ROBERT A. LOVETT,
Acting Secretary of State.

[F. R. Doc. 47-10701; Filed, Dec. 2, 1947; 12:08 p. m.]

Sanibel National Wildlife Refuge was created on December 1, 1945, when the Fish and Wildlife Service, the Florida Trustees of the Internal Improvement Trust Fund, and the Florida Board of Education executed a lease document. This agreement gave the Service management of 2,296 acres of state-owned mangrove habitat on Sanibel for refuge purposes. Contrary to some published sources, the refuge was not created by a presidential executive order. Later, using the Migratory Bird Treaty Act, Pres. Harry Truman issued Proclamation 2758, which made all of Sanibel and some of the adjacent waters a Closed Area. The pursuing, hunting, taking, or killing of migratory birds would no longer be permitted within the Proclamation boundary. Pictured is the page from the *Federal Register*, dated December 3, 1947, when the closure became effective. (USFWS.)

Darling and his allies attained their objective when Sanibel National Wildlife Refuge came to life with a stroke of a pen in 1945, when the state lands were leased by the Fish and Wildlife Service. It would be another 50 years before the "child" of those early advocates reached maturity. Totally delighted with the achievement, Darling penned the above piece of art to celebrate the refuge's birth, in 1945. (Andrea and Kip Koss.)

Settlers arriving on the islands consumed every kind of edible living creature, including white ibis, pictured above, and gopher tortoises. Known as curlews, ibis were shot as they arrived at their roosts at dusk. Subsistence take of wildlife waned after creation of the refuge, but illegal hunting of these birds and migratory waterfowl continued into the 1960s. The waters within the refuge boundary supported significant populations of wintering waterfowl such as the pair of blue-winged teal pictured below. These birds were also heavily hunted prior to the refuge's creation. (Both, Sanibel-Captiva Nature Calendar.)

Dewilton "Jake" Stokes (1909–1989) appears with a large eastern diamondback rattlesnake he found swimming in San Carlos Bay. In 1947, Jake was the first local resident laborer-patrolman to be hired directly by the Fish and Wildlife Service. He only served part-time for about a year, and was later a fishing and shelling guide. In the photograph below, taken in 1956, he is at the wheel of his boat on the way to a favorite shelling bed in the Gulf 12 miles to the northwest of Knapp's Point, to dredge live junonias, lion's paws, spiny oysters, and other rare collectable species. Jake's former daughter-in-law, Edythe Stokes (1928–2005), would become an employee of J.N. "Ding" Darling National Wildlife Refuge in 1970. (Both, Marty Stokes.)

The private retreat "Ding" Darling built in 1941 in which to spend his Captiva winters is seen in the above photograph. He called it his Fish House, and claimed it was "the last resort of free men." When he did not wish to be disturbed Darling would raise a drawbridge. In the image below, Darling was so fond of his Fish House that he rendered the pen and ink of the building as he saw it himself. This sketch was used as a letterhead on his personal stationery. Note the cartoonist penned himself, relaxing with a fishing pole, on the top deck at the left railing. The unique drawbridge is in the up position. (Both, Andrea and Kip Koss.)

"Ding" Darling (left) and his good friend and favorite fishing guide, Belton Johnson, are enjoying some quiet time together fishing in Roosevelt Channel, between Buck Key and Captiva Island. Belton (1896–1986) spent a career as a popular charter-fishing captain, and was a well-respected member of the island communities. (Andrea and Kip Koss.)

## PROPERTY OWNERS

*PETITION TO CLOSE, BY EXECUTIVE ORDER,* all shooting, trapping or other molestation of birds and wild life on Sanibel and Captiva islands and adjacent island rookeries and feeding grounds, subject to the management and supervision of the U. S. Fish & Wild Life Service of the U. S. Department of Interior.

Signature _J. N. Darling_

Address _Captiva,_
_Fla._

"Ding" Darling gave his full energy and used his national reputation to launch a drive to protect the wildlife values of the sister islands of Sanibel and Captiva. This is his personally-signed petition, among several hundred others that island property owners submitted to the Fish and Wildlife Service in support of establishing a national wildlife refuge on Sanibel. (Author.)

32

Refuge Manager/Pilot William D. "Tommy" Wood, (1903–1990), was born in Ozona, Florida, and first soloed in an aircraft in 1927. During World War II he flew Navy PBY seaplanes. After the war, Tommy took a Laborer-Patrolman position at Key West and Great White Heron National Wildlife Refuges. The aircraft pictured with him above is his personal seaplane. In the photograph below, Tommy is with the government-owned Piper Super Cub N-757 in 1960. Initially, William C. "Bill" Lehmann was the patrolman responsible for the island refuges. His demeanor did not meet "Ding" Darling's concept of a refuge officer and Darling pressured Lehmann's supervisors to replace him. While Jake Stokes filled in, the search continued. The next candidate was Claude Lowe from Tavernier, but he resigned rather than transfer to Sanibel permanently. Tommy was offered the job and he and his wife, Louise, relocated to Sanibel. "Ding" Darling and Tommy became fast friends and Lehmann became a US Game Management Agent. (Above, James Pickens; below, author.)

THE LAST OF THE "TOY" DEER
OF THE FLORIDA KEYS

In 1950, South Florida Refuges manager Gerald Baker enlisted "Ding" Darling's help and launched the fight to save the Key deer of the middle Florida Keys. With the above cartoon, Darling helped the national effort to save an individual species. When inspired, he departed from the broader conservation issues he was usually associated with, like saving wetlands and waterfowl. The Key deer's population was down to 30 animals when the Fish and Wildlife Service intervened. Today, the National Key Deer Refuge, established in 1957, contains 8,542 acres and about 800 Key deer. ("Ding" Darling Wildlife Society.)

PHONY!
I COULD
DRAW A
BETTER PICTURE
OF TOMMY WOOD
THAN THAT MYSELF
AND I CAN'T DRAW
AT ALL!

FROM
"DING" DARLING
ONE OF HIS MOST APPRECIATIVE
AND GRATEFUL FRIENDS.

A MERRY CHRISTMAS TO TOMMY WOOD
THE MODERN ST. FRANCIS OF SANIBEL REFUGE
FROM ALL US BIRDS AND BEASTIES.

This cartoon is a Christmas card that was given to Tommy and Louise Wood by "Ding" Darling, in 1950. This is a rare piece of Darling art, because it was rendered in full color as opposed to his usual medium, black and white pen and ink. Today, a replication hangs on the wall in the mock-up of "Ding" Darling's studio in the refuge's Education Center. (Author.)

Darling was no slouch when it came to expressing his views about hollow promises and the trend to politicize wildlife conservation. The above cartoon was titled "Don't Say it—Sign it!" Its message is as appropriate today as it was in the 1930s. ("Ding" Darling Wildlife Society.)

# Three

# THE LIGHTHOUSE YEARS

After negotiating a lease with the Coast Guard, the Fish and Wildlife Service established refuge headquarters at Point Ybel. The Coast Guard continued to control the still operational, but automated, light tower. Tommy and Louise Wood moved into Quarters 1, and one of their bedrooms became the refuge office. Quarters 2 was rented to James Hager, of the Florida State Board of Health, who was on Sanibel to conduct mosquito studies. Later, private citizen Paul Stahlin and his family lived there for two years. In 1955, the refuge built a workshop on the grounds, and a large concrete cistern was installed behind Quarters 3.

Potable water was critical, and had to be rationed. Quarters 1 and 3 had wooden and concrete cisterns, but Quarters 2 used a rusted metal tank, located between Quarters 1 and 2, for a cistern. In 1956, Stahlin had a shallow well point driven, and to everyone's surprise, the water was potable. A jet pump with a pressure tank distributed water from this well into the three buildings. The system had a bypass valve so the Quarters 3 cistern could be maintained at a full level and drawn from in emergencies. This worked until Hurricane Donna flooded the point on September 10, 1960, and seawater ruined the quality of the well. In 1962, preparatory to building a base at Point Ybel, (which was never built), the Coast Guard drilled a 475-foot-deep artesian well, and although a little saline, it served the quarters for non-potable purposes. In 1966, the refuge connected to water distributed by the new Island Water Association, and the station's ongoing water problems were solved.

In 1976, after 27 years, the Service decided that public recreational uses at Point Ybel were incompatible with refuge objectives. The decision was made to relinquish Point Ybel and relocate headquarters. A new maintenance center, on Sanibel-Captiva Road, was completed in 1980. Two years later, a new administrative office and visitor center were finished, and the Fish and Wildlife Service left Point Ybel. The City of Sanibel negotiated with the Coast Guard and assumed management of the lighthouse parcel as a city park in 1982. The city formally acquired the property in 2010.

The Sanibel Lighthouse is a hurricane-resistant, pyramidal structure made mostly of wrought iron. The center of the light is 98 feet above sea level. Originally kerosene-fueled and equipped with a rotating third-order Fresnel lens, the beacon was visible 18 miles offshore. It was electrified in 1962. Sanibel Light is a landfall light, erected to guide shipping traffic to Port Punta Rassa. This photograph was taken in about 1935. (Francis Bailey.)

This 1942 photograph captures Lighthouse Quarters 2 with its 4,000-gallon cistern and downspouts in place. The station's water supply fell from the heavens and was piped from the cistern directly into the kitchens. This cistern was washed away in a 1947 hurricane, but water from the cistern at Quarters 1 was consumed by refuge personnel until 1963, when it was discovered to be contaminated with asbestos fibers from the roof shingles. (US Coast Guard.)

Water was pumped into a 1,000-gallon tank atop a tower next to this ground-level cistern; it was gravity-fed to the quarters and available for fire suppression. A similar high tank received pumped brackish water from a shallow well point, and this supplied the quarter's toilets. Modern toilets were not installed until 1923—before that, outhouses were used. These were located on the porches close to the elevated cisterns. The stairways provided access to the light tower directly from the porches. (US Coast Guard.)

Point Ybel was managed by the Sanibel Refuge when this photograph was taken in 1950. The small leaning tower on the beach in front of the light tower, and the cottage to the right, were built in 1942 for use by the Coast Guard beach patrol contingent stationed on Sanibel during World War II. The Coast Guard's rules, which separated its branches, prohibited patrol personnel from using the light tower as an observation post. (USFWS.)

The above photograph was taken in about 1950. The original staircases leading from each porch to the light tower were removed the next year. The Hager family is gathered on the porch of Lighthouse Quarters 2. Erosion at Point Ybel is at its worst, and the Gulf of Mexico is under the building. The photograph below captures the headquarters in 1958, from the refuge's floatplane. The ferry landing is visible at the top, and the small boat basin on the bay was developed in 1955 by Ernest Kinzie, ferry operator. A 10-foot alligator that lived in the basin caught and killed Tommy Wood's dog, a boxer that protected headquarters when he was away in the field. The road through the center was built by the Lee County Mosquito Control District when their Sanibel ditching program started. (Both, USFWS.)

*Old Coast Guard Tower, Sanibel Island, Fla.*

By 1948, the wartime observation post was so damaged by hurricanes and undermined by beach erosion that it was leaning precariously. This postcard, by artist Gladys Childs, captures the tower's condition in 1960. The decision was made to burn it before someone climbed it and got hurt. Periodically, its concrete footers are still uncovered by currents at Point Ybel. (Gladys Childs.)

Refuge headquarters appears in 1967. The metal cistern is visible between the quarters, as are the elevated tanks. The raised tank to the right received brackish water, and the other tank's water was pumped from the ground-level cistern until it was disconnected in the early 1950s. The height allowed gravity distribution of water to the quarters. By 1959, barn owls took up residence in the dry left-hand tank and raised families each year until the tanks and towers were removed in 1969. As a condition of employment, refuge staff members were required to live in the lighthouse quarters. Rent, withheld from their biweekly paychecks, was nine dollars per month, and they paid their own electric bills. There were no private telephones until 1962 and no air conditioning until 1968. The office in Quarters 1 did have a telephone—for official business only. (Author.)

The permanent refuge staff is pictured in the photograph below in the days before uniforms. Tommy Wood (left) and Charles LeBuff are pictured outside the office in January 1959. The image above captures the refuge headquarters site in 1960. Noteworthy is the maintenance of the grounds. The lighthouse compound was kept free of vegetation to reduce fire danger and to let wind help curtail thirsty mosquitoes. On some mornings, the window screens on the leeward side of both quarters would be black with the insects—literally so thickly matted that they could not be seen through. (Above, USFWS; below, Jean LeBuff.)

This cottage, photographed in 1942, housed the Coast Guard's wartime beach patrol unit. It contained a kitchen, bathroom, living room, and two bedrooms. It was elevated on concrete pilings, but hurricanes in the 1940s filled in around them. This dwelling became a guest cottage, a vacation retreat for Service employees. In 1959, the rental fee was two dollars per night, with a one-week maximum stay. In 1967, an employee from the Washington office arrived early, before staff checked the cottage, and found odiferous bait shrimp in the refrigerator, which had been left unplugged by the previous vacationer. Not being very objective, he complained directly to the regional director. After that, regional refuge supervisor Lawrence Givens ordered the rental unit shut down. In the photograph below from 1969, the Sanibel Refuge Motel is being razed. (Above, US Coast Guard; below, author.)

When the refuge office was opened in 1949, the road leading to the lighthouse compound followed the ridge paralleling the Gulf beach. The road was moved to the bay-side of Point Ybel in 1970. In the above photograph, manager Tommy Wood stands near the entrance sign in 1958. The vehicle is a surplus military jeep, the workhorse of the refuge's two-vehicle fleet. In the photograph below, staff member Charles LeBuff and his son Charles "Chuck" LeBuff III stand near the upgraded headquarters entrance sign in 1971. (Above, USFWS; below, Harry Rogers.)

The Coast Guard pier, pictured above in 1965, was transformed into a public fishing pier. The pier had to be rebuilt from the pilings up after Hurricane Donna shredded it in 1960. Piling deterioration led to the unannounced closing of this pier in 1971. This action raised such a public outcry that the Service designed a new pier, but actual construction was financed by the Sanibel-Captiva Chamber of Commerce and Lee County. The replacement (below) was completed in 1972 and is positioned 300 feet to the west of the original pier. It has since undergone major renovations by the city using the same basic footprint. (Both, USFWS.)

In the early days, the refuge staff was often the recipient of orphaned and injured wildlife. Without an island care facility, the more seriously injured animals brought to headquarters were humanely euthanized. An organization to handle such patients was not conceived until 1972, when the Clinic for the Rehabilitation of Wildlife was launched by islanders Jesse Dugger and Shirley Walter. In the photograph above, Leslie LeBuff (left) and her brother Chuck admire two orphaned burrowing owls they cared for in 1964. In the 1969 photograph at right, temporary refuge employee Raymond Carner holds a baby manatee that a staff member rescued on Captiva. No marine exhibit or public aquarium contacted would accept this orphaned manatee. Therefore, without any other viable options, the LeBuff family kept the animal alive for 64 days. (Above, author; right, USFWS.)

The refuge supports a variety of small mammals. According to historic accounts, Sanibel once supported a herd of whitetail deer, which drowned during flooding in the 1926 hurricane. Pictured at left is a bobcat photographed in the Bailey Tract. Like the deer, bobcats were extirpated from Sanibel by 1926. Releases of rehabilitated mainland bobcats on Sanibel by the Clinic for the Care and Rehabilitation of Wildlife in the mid-1970s resulted in this predator's reintroduction into the island's ecosystems. The photograph below captures a family of curious raccoons along Wildlife Drive. Raccoons are abundant on the islands, and in the summer, they move to the Gulf beach to prey on incubating sea turtle eggs. Raccoons negatively impact the nesting success of sea turtles and have contributed to their decline. (Left, Sanibel-Captiva Nature Calendar; below, Gerri Much.)

From 1959 until 1971, Charles LeBuff managed nuisance alligators on Sanibel. Alligators that he captured and relocated were marked with tags furnished by the Sanibel-Captiva Audubon Society, as part of an alligator study that LeBuff conducted when off-duty. Over 500 island alligators were tagged and recorded during this time. In the photograph at right from 1962, LeBuff is sporting the new Fish and Wildlife Service's taupe-colored uniform. George Weymouth, who is pictured below, was a temporary refuge worker in 1971. He also assisted in the alligator management program, and in this photograph from the early 1970s, he has captured an adult alligator that was soon to be measured, tagged, and relocated. (Right, Laymond Hardy; below, author.)

The bull alligator pictured above is basking along Wildlife Drive. When mosquito control brought permanent surface water to Sanibel, the alligator population soared. In the 1960s, alligators were impacted by poachers, as the value of their hides skyrocketed. On one occasion on October 26, 1965, near the Bailey Tract, a refuge officer discovered the remains of 23 alligators, all missing their hides. The rare American crocodile in the photograph below was first observed on the refuge in 1979. Native crocodiles are timid and thus less dangerous than their alligator cousins are. Before the feeding of alligators was banned on Sanibel in 1974, many alligators lost their natural fear of man from being fed. Unfortunately, illegal feeders persisted, and there have been two human fatalities from alligator attacks on Sanibel in recent years. (Both, Sanibel-Captiva Nature Calendar.)

At first, the crocodile was very shy and afraid of people, but soon grew accustomed to an audience and in the winters, chose to haul out and bask along Wildlife Drive on cold days. The animal was discovered to be female when she was observed building nests and laying eggs—which never hatched. Over time, until her death in early 2010, she seemed to enjoy her solitary fame. In the photograph, a group of refuge visitors crowds a barricade—they have the crocodile in sight. (USFWS.)

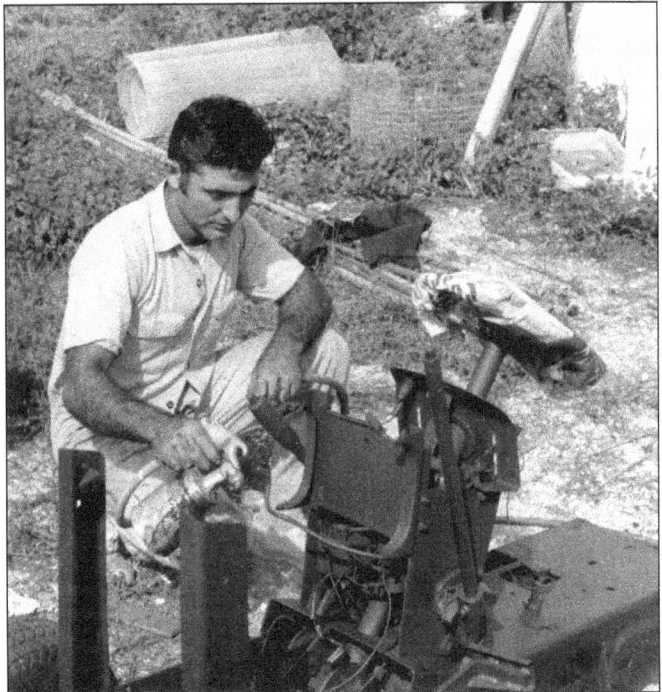

Robert "Bob" Sabatino, shown in this 1966 photograph, was employed at the refuge during summers only. In the winter season, he was too busy booking charters for his popular live shelling and fishing trips. By the early 1970s, Bob had developed such a high reputation as a guide that the demands of his growing and repeat client base prevented him from accepting further seasonal work at the refuge. (USFWS.)

In 1976, independent naturalists began having an important role in environmental education on the refuge. These profit-making "guides" operated under refuge-issued, fee-based Special Use Permits. Pictured from left to right are Mark "Bird" Westall, who operated canoe trip adventures; George Weymouth, who was popular for his birding tours; George Campbell, who led general natural history tours; and Griffing Bancroft (1907–1999), a former CBS Radio commentator, who was a birding guide. Westall later became the refuge's first volunteer. (USFWS.)

# Four

# EARLY REFUGE MANAGEMENT

America's first national wildlife refuge was Pelican Island Reservation, originally a five-acre rookery island in the Indian River Lagoon on Florida's east coast. Created by Pres. Theodore Roosevelt on March 14, 1903, Pelican Island was initially under the control of the US Department of Agriculture's Bureau of Biological Survey. Over the next few decades, other presidents authorized additional migratory bird reservations across the nation. They were formally renamed, and have since been called national wildlife refuges, as authorized by a proclamation issued by Pres. Franklin Roosevelt on July 30, 1940. The refuge system was also transferred from the Department of Agriculture to the Interior Department's new Fish and Wildlife Service in 1940.

In 1938, the national wildlife refuges of coastal southern Florida were unstaffed islands and administratively combined as the Florida Islands National Wildlife Refuges. They were periodically patrolled by laborer-patrolman William Lehmann (1910–1982), from his office in Mango, near Tampa Bay. The areas included Cedar Key, Anclote River, Indian Key, Fort De Soto, Passage Key, Island Bay, Pine Island, Matlacha Pass, and the Caloosahatchee National Wildlife Refuges, all on the Gulf Coast. Lehmann occasionally traveled to the east coast and patrolled Brevard, Pelican Island, and Matanzas NWRs.

Later, other Florida islands were added to the complex administered from Sanibel. The most recent to be established was Egmont Key NWR, a beautiful and historic barrier island at the mouth of Tampa Bay. It was created in 1974 and was grouped into a small complex known as Tampa Bay Refuges, which includes Pinellas and Passage Key Refuges. These were temporarily staffed by an assistant manager between 1980 and 1983. In 1984, responsibility for the Tampa Bay Refuges was transferred to Chassahowitzka NWR, near Crystal River. The J.N. "Ding" Darling NWR Complex is responsible for several satellite refuges, which consist of scores of islands, some of them major colonial bird rookeries. These refuges are Island Bay, Pine Island, Matlacha Pass, and Caloosahatchee NWRs. None of these satellite refuges are staffed.

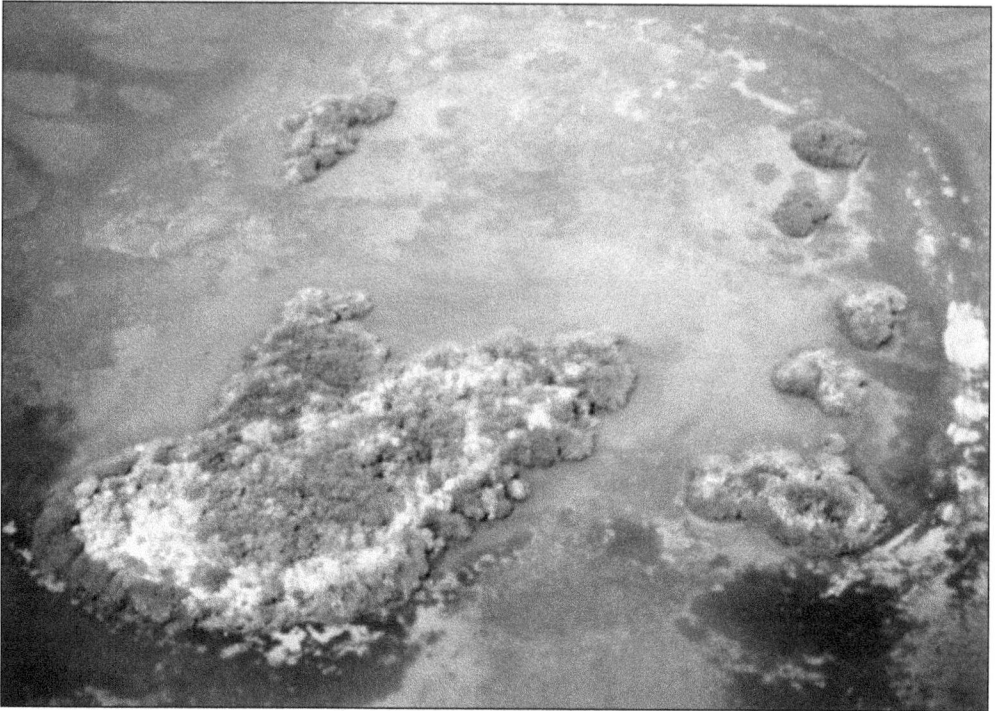

Paul Kroegel (1864–1948) is pictured below at Pelican Island Reservation. German-born Kroegel was the nation's first national wildlife refuge manager. On April 1, 1903, two weeks after Pres. Theodore Roosevelt created this reservation, Kroegel was commissioned as a federal warden and assigned to protect the birds at Pelican Island. He held the post until 1926, when funding for his one-dollar-per-month salary was abruptly cut off by Congress. His services were no longer needed after brown pelicans abandoned Pelican Island and relocated to Mosquito Lagoon, where Brevard NWR was established in 1925. The photograph above shows a Gulf Coast counterpart of Pelican Island. Pictured is Bird Island, part of Pine Island National Wildlife Refuge. It became a national wildlife refuge only five years after Pelican Island did. Historically, it has been one of the most important colonial nesting bird roosts/rookeries on Florida's Gulf Coast. (Both, USFWS.)

During severe droughts, the bottom of the Sanibel Slough was exposed and would become temporarily vegetated before the summer rains arrived. Only a few scattered alligator holes held surface water until summer precipitation again flooded the wetlands. The above photograph was taken in the Bailey Tract and is oriented southward, where a single row of Australian pines is visible. These trees were growing along a Gulf-front road that once connected Casa Ybel Hotel with Island Inn, before Hurricane Donna removed the road in 1960. In the photograph below is Stewart Pond at maximum drought in 1950. This pond was located in what today is the Chateaux Sur Mer subdivision, on the Gulf beach in the western section of Sanibel. Like other larger ponds on Sanibel, it was leased by the refuge because of its value to migrating and resident birds. (Both, USFWS.)

The photograph at left was taken in March 1950, next to the Bailey Tract's Mangrove Head. Using 43 blasting caps, 625 sticks of dynamite were detonated in an attempt to create a pothole and expose enough surface water to support minnows through the dry season, prey for fish and wildlife. The photograph below was taken immediately after the mud settled. When the next rainy season arrived, wandering alligators discovered and occupied the blasted depressions, and over time, their use kept the depressions wallowed-out and made this pothole experiment a success. Eventually, a few 12-foot alligators established territories here and stayed put until, one by one, they fell victim to poachers in the early 1960s. (Both, USFWS.)

In 1954, manager Wood released 49 pig frogs into the Bailey Tract. This 100-acre parcel was the first land purchased on Sanibel by the Service. This frog, the legs of which are edible, was not indigenous to the islands. The specimens were collected at Loxahatchee National Wildlife Refuge for release on Sanibel to enhance wildlife food diversity. The pig frog is now common on the island. Their pig-like grunting is often incorrectly identified as sounds made by alligators. ("Ding" Darling Wildlife Society.)

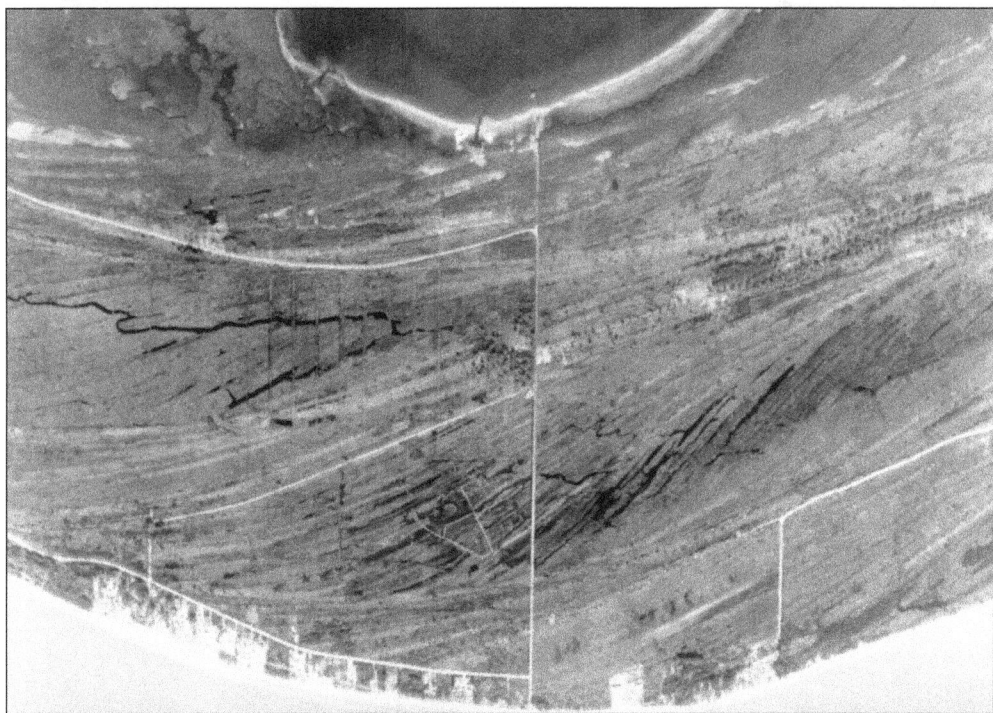

This photograph from about 1955 was taken above mid-island. The vertical road at center is Tarpon Bay Road, and the triangle-shaped development to its left (west) is the Bailey Tract. The mostly undisturbed portions of Sanibel Slough and the course of the Sanibel River are clearly visible. The road to the right of Tarpon Bay Road is Casa Ybel Road. The roads are not connected. The sod airstrip at Casa Ybel Hotel had recently been created. It would be closed in 1979. (James Pickens.)

This 1960 photograph captures the Sanibel Slough being channelized by the Lee County Mosquito Control District. The sand-surfaced Rabbit Road is the vertical road to the right, and the development in the center foreground is the West Rocks subdivision on West Gulf Drive. The slough and adjacent wetlands produced world-record numbers of salt marsh mosquitoes. In 1950, near the Sanibel ferry landing, a device known as a New Jersey light trap captured 364,672 of these nuisance mosquitoes in just one night. (US Natural Resources Conservation Service.)

This tower, known as the Bird Tower, was erected in the Bailey Tract in 1954. It became popular among bird watchers because it presented a panoramic vista of the Sanibel Slough. Each evening, thousands of white ibis, wheeling in aerial perfection, arrived to spend the night roosting in the nearby Mangrove Head. Over time, plant transition resulted in the tract's wetlands being invaded by cattail. Darling's artesian well was a few yards away from this tower. This well was plugged and the tower razed in 1976. The photograph below of the new Seaplane Canal and the aircraft's home base was taken in 1961. The road in the foreground leaves paved Tarpon Bay Road and meets the canal near a power pole. The ramp and dolly used to winch the plane from the canal for dry storage is located to the left of the pole. Interestingly, the cattails have not altered the Bailey Tract at this point. (Both, USFWS.)

In 1970, an oil spill impacted Tampa Bay, and refuge employees were dispatched to evaluate it. In the above photograph, Marvin Hurdle, assistant manager of South Florida National Wildlife Refuges, is inspecting a pool of oil near Bush Key, of Pinellas NWR. The photograph below documents the remains of a scaup duck covered with oil. Between 1977 and 1983, two additional spills occurred in Tampa Bay. The worst of these occurred in 1978, when 952 barrels of No. 6 oil were accidentally discharged into upper Tampa Bay. (Both, USFWS.)

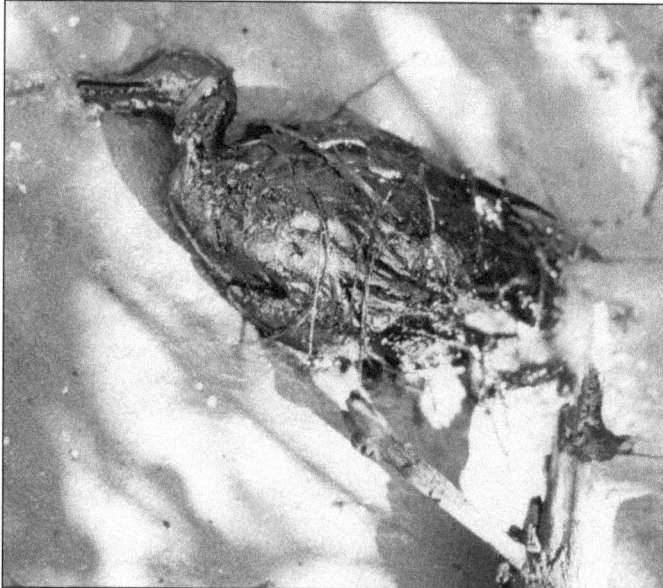

Enforcement of refuge regulations was sometimes difficult. On September 26, 1962, while on an inspection flight, Tommy Wood and South Florida Refuges manager Bill Julian discovered a major trespass on Cash Mound, part of Island Bay National Wildlife Refuge, in Charlotte County. As shown in the image above, the Charlotte Oyster Company had put a dragline ashore and was digging shell from the ancient Calusa Indian mound. The shell was being barged to nearby leased bottoms and dumped overboard to develop commercial oyster beds. This case went through the federal court system, but in the end, attorney general Robert Kennedy made the decision not to prosecute, and the vandals never went to trial for wreaking major damage on an important archaeological site. Like other refuge units during this period, the mound was identified with boundary signs, including posted penalties (below). (Above, USFWS; below, author.)

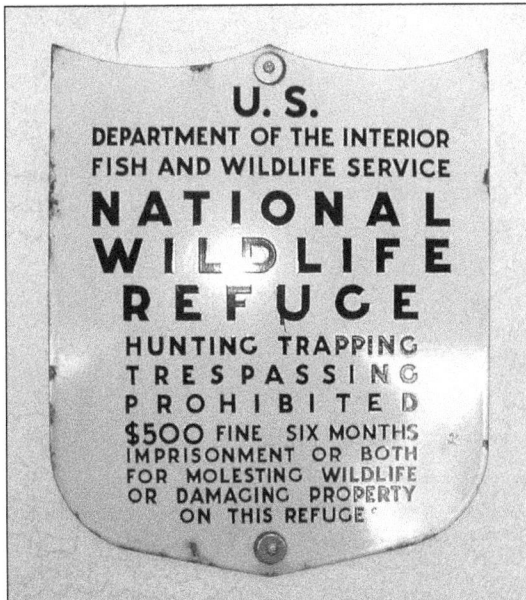

U. S.
DEPARTMENT OF THE INTERIOR
FISH AND WILDLIFE SERVICE

NATIONAL
WILDLIFE
REFUGE

HUNTING TRAPPING
TRESPASSING
PROHIBITED

$500 FINE SIX MONTHS
IMPRISONMENT OR BOTH
FOR MOLESTING WILDLIFE
OR DAMAGING PROPERTY
ON THIS REFUGE

Boundary posting on Sanibel and the satellite refuge islands is a constant effort. In the photograph at left from 1985, Charles LeBuff (left) and Richard Blackburn are jetting in a post with boundary and wilderness area signs attached on Bull Key, part of Island Bay NWR. The headquarters staff of the South Florida Refuges Complex, based at Loxahatchee NWR, is pictured in the photograph below in 1969. From left to right are administrative assistant Raymond Brown, manager John Eadie, manager trainee Ralph Keel, maintenance man Ira Westbrook, mechanic Even Rude, assistant manager Marvin Hurdle, and outdoor recreation planner Ed Murchek. (Left, USFWS; below, John Eadie, USFWS.)

Following Tommy Wood's retirement, on January 9, 1971, Robert "Bob" Barber, an assistant manager at the National Bison Range in Montana, was selected as his replacement. Bob assumed the position on April 19, 1971, and he and his wife, Julie, and their two sons moved into new and remodeled refuge housing at the former Dewey's Marina on Tarpon Bay. Pictured in 1973 are, from left to right, refuge manager Robert Barber, visual information specialist Charlotte Shea, clerk-typist Edythe Stokes, biological technician Charles LeBuff, and assistant refuge manager Glenn Carowan. Manager Barber transferred to the Atlanta Regional Office on October 28, 1973. (USFWS.)

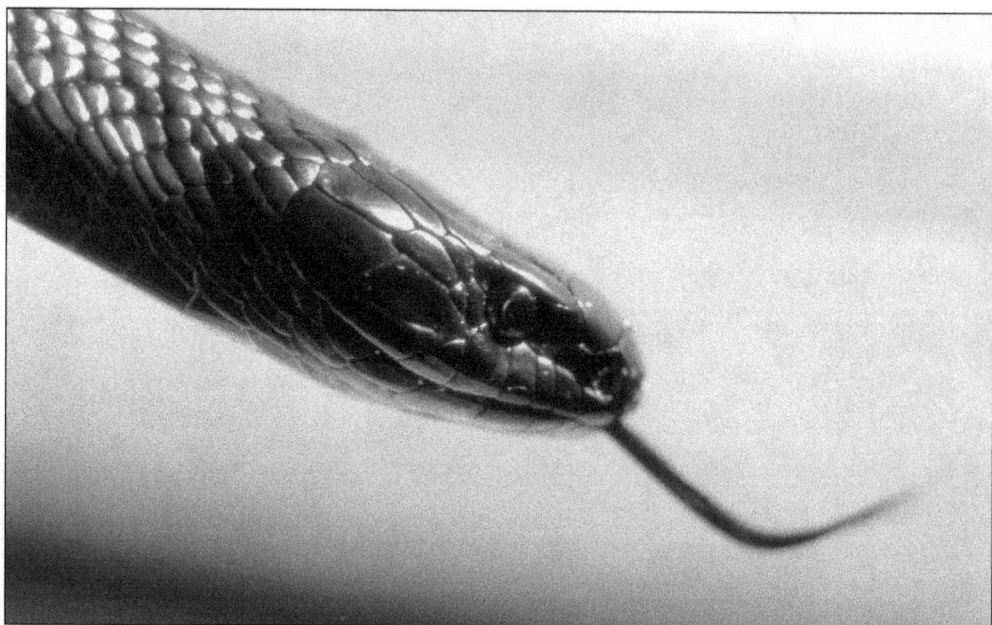

At one time, the endangered eastern indigo snake was common on Sanibel. Pictured above, these are the largest nonvenomous snake in North America. On Sanibel, they frequented the uplands and sought refuge in gopher tortoise burrows. By 2000, the indigo snake was considered extirpated on Sanibel, mostly because of deadly road traffic that often hit and killed the big snakes as they crossed island roads and development of their high-ground habitat for home sites. Some were even collected alive for the pet trade. Gopher tortoises, pictured below, were once common and unprotected, and important in the diet of early islanders. (Above, author; below, Chris Lechowicz.)

A severe red tide impacted the islands during the summer of 1971. In this photograph, dead fish are heaped on the bay beach just west of the refuge fishing pier. Every nook and cranny of beach and mangroves were thick with decomposing fish and other marine organisms. The dying red-tide-causing organism, *Karenia brevis*, releases a peculiar odor. It mixes with the stench of decaying marine life to form a foul-smelling airborne aerosol that is carried to shore by the sea breeze. Unable to cope with the ghastly smell, residents were trapped indoors, and visitors were driven away, much to the chagrin of the business community. The refuge provided a disposal site at Point Ybel when Lee County sent a fleet of dump trucks, heavy equipment, and clean-up crews to the island. Road graders scraped the beach and front-end loaders lifted hundreds of tons of the dead creatures into trucks. They were hauled to refuge headquarters and dumped into their mass grave. (Author.)

J.N. "Ding" Darling NWR participated in the Youth Conservation Corps (YCC) program in 1977. Michael "Bill" Lubich, from Rice's Landing, Pennsylvania, was the YCC crew leader in 1977 and 1979. In 1981, he was selected as the refuge's YCC Camp Director. The YCC was assigned projects on the refuge, freeing staff to complete other assignments critical to the management of the refuge. In the above photograph, the 1977 YCC crew is repairing the roof of the refuge shop at Point Ybel. An important aspect of the YCC program was regular classroom sessions, which provided enrollees elements of environmental education. To their delight, they discovered the program was not just labor-intensive work, but also fun. In the photograph below, taken in 1977, YCC enrollees are conducting water quality analysis along the refuge's Wildlife Drive. (Both, Michael Lubich.)

Merritt Island NWR assistant manager Glen Bond became manager of J.N. "Ding" Darling NWR on December 13, 1973. The staff, photographed in 1975, consists of, from left to right, refuge manager Glen Bond, biological technician Charles LeBuff, clerk-typist Edythe Stokes, and assistant refuge manager Patrick Hagan. During Glen Bond's tenure on Sanibel, the refuge launched a pest plant control program. Later, refuge manager Del Pierce made a commitment to wage war against undesirable exotic plants. The worst of these were the noxious Australian pine and Brazilian pepper. In the photograph at right, a sapling Australian pine is being girdled and the herbicide 2,4-Dichlorophenoxyacetic acid (2,4-D) applied to the cuts from the spray bottle. (Both, USFWS.)

The scope of pest plant control expanded during the 1980s. The program included the satellite refuges where Australian pines and Brazilian pepper had outcompeted desirable native plants. In the above photograph, Australian pines are being mechanically removed on a spoil island to enhance ground-nesting seabird habitat. The photograph below shows the completed job. (Both, USFWS.)

In 1974, the refuge manager decided that sea turtle conservation was no longer part of the refuge's mission. Charles LeBuff continued his work privately, when off-duty, and was regularly joined on the beach at night by assistant refuge manager Glenn Carowan, and later Patrick Hagan, during their free time. In this 1973 photograph are, from left to right, Jim Anholt, Warren Boutchia, and Glenn Carowan. In 1968, the sea turtle conservation program was formalized and became Caretta Research, Inc. Its purposes were broadened, and soon, a large group of volunteers were enlisted. At first, the new organization was sponsored by the Sanibel-Captiva Conservation Foundation (SCCF), but in 1973 the all-volunteer group became an independent, tax-exempt organization. In 1991, Caretta Research, Inc. was dissolved and SCCF took over primary responsibilities for sea turtles and their conservation on the islands. (Author.)

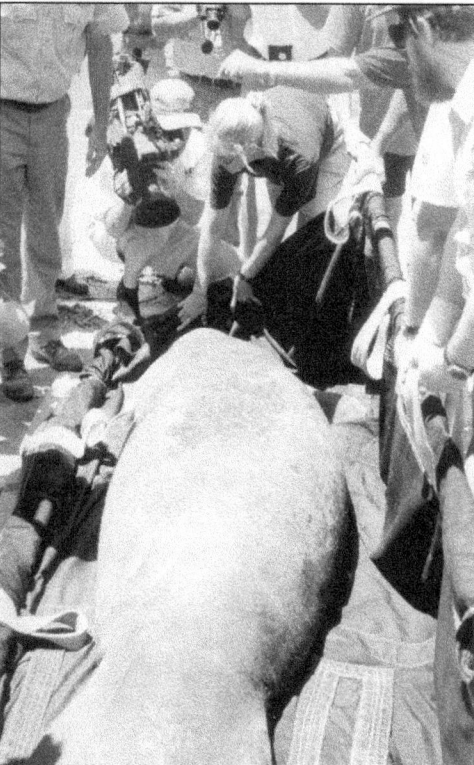

Manatees, also called sea cows, have increased in local waters since the creation of the refuge, but their increase is due to an unnatural factor. A power plant on the Caloosahatchee, east of Fort Myers, discharges heated water, and this provides area manatees a cold-weather refuge, which reduces their hypothermic mortality. Sightings are usually confined to an instant-long glimpse of the tip of a manatee's nose as it surfaces to breath, as in the above photograph. Refuge law enforcement staff participated with other agencies and enforced seasonal manatee speed zones in area waterways and occasionally rescued injured sea cows. In the photograph at left, an injured manatee is being released back into Tarpon Bay (where it was rescued) after it was rehabilitated by Sea World Orlando. (Above, Rob Jess, USFWS; left, USFWS.)

# Five

# THE WILDLIFE DRIVE

The state-owned lands on the northern side of Sanibel, which land speculators were coveting in the 1940s, consist of a myriad of shallow tidal bayous dominated by red mangrove forests. This estuarine ecosystem is a vital nursery for a wide variety of marine life, such as shrimp, crabs, and fishes—all of which has important economic value for commercial and recreational fisheries. The shallow grass and mud flats harbor a host of wildlife prey species, which feed both migratory and resident birds.

This is the area that concerned "Ding" Darling and motivated him to successfully blockade the State of Florida's Trustees of the Internal Improvement Trust Fund when they considered selling lands owned by the people of Florida to private real estate developers.

What has become a popular Wildlife Drive actually started out as a weapon in the war against mosquitoes. No one expected, at the time, that it would become a major component in developing a lasting tribute to J.N. "Ding" Darling. Biological mosquito control, through the ditching program in the Sanibel Slough, worked because it produced permanent surface water, resulting in year-round survival of mosquito larvae–eating fishes. However, the tidal flats in the refuge continued to produce overwhelming numbers of salt marsh mosquitoes. When the Mosquito Control District's draglines were completing their mission in the Sanibel Slough, refuge manager Tommy Wood asked district director T. Wayne Miller to move his equipment into the mangroves and develop a water impoundment to reduce reproduction of the salt marsh mosquitoes. They agreed that all the spoil would be cast in the center, between the borrow ditches, and not on both sides, as was done in the slough. The fact that this dike would provide public access to the tidal area was a secondary purpose, but Wood probably had that in the back of his mind. The "Ding" Darling Memorial Sanctuary Committee (established to honor Darling after his death) was overjoyed that something was going to happen on the ground. They appointed refuge manager Tommy Wood to be their honorary chief engineer.

'BYE NOW—IT'S BEEN WONDERFUL KNOWING YOU.

The day after his death, the *Des Moines Register* published Darling's final cartoon. He originally created this following a serious illness in 1959 and presented the cartoon to his editor with the understanding that it would be published immediately after his death. As his spiritual form leaves his studio, Darling leaves behind an immense body of work. His life's major interests and accomplishments are represented in this cartoon. ("Ding" Darling Wildlife Society.)

Within days after his death, island friends of Darling met and discussed the best approach to honor the man. The J.N. "Ding" Darling Memorial Sanctuary Committee was born out of this grim meeting. Darling's daughter, Mary Koss, telephoned refuge manager Tommy Wood from Iowa and insisted he serve on the committee. Emmy Lu Lewis (1904–1990), pictured here, who never met Darling personally, was selected to chair his memorial committee. (Sanibel Historical Museum and Village.)

Sanibel is photographed looking eastward in 1958. From this perspective, Clam Bayou and Silver Key are in the foreground. Blind Pass cuts through the beach at center right, far from its current location, and Point Ybel is in the far distance. In 1943, Darling discovered that about 3,000 acres of the Sanibel mangrove forest were going to be sold by the state to a Tampa real estate developer. Darling wrote Florida governor Spessard Holland and informed him of the proposed national wildlife refuge that was to include these very lands. The governor quickly withdrew the land from the sale schedule. The Service would acquire fee title to this same Sanibel land 20 years later, after a real estate exchange with the State of Florida, for FWS land the state wanted to use for park purposes. (Betty Anholt.)

In 1962, two draglines started work in the tidal mangroves of the Darling Tract. The one pictured above was operated by Colon Moore. The other machine was moved to another project after a few weeks, and Moore continued his work alone. When finished with the main dike in 1966, he moved his machine and started work on the south dike (now called Indigo Trail). However, when adjacent property owners threatened legal challenges to this dike's alignment, work was halted. And that is why the Indigo Trail has a dead end. In the photograph below, Moore sits in his dragline, which rests on thick wooden mats to prevent the machine from sinking into the mud. He first dug one spoil canal to create one side of the dike and then turned his dragline around and started back on the other side. Periodically, a bulldozer would arrive and level the piles of sand. This gave Moore vehicle access to his machine for easier refueling. (Both, author.)

This 1990 photograph shows most of Wildlife Drive. The opening in the mangroves to the lower right leads into Hardworking Bayou. Diagonally up and to the left is a triangle of white beach that Tommy Wood named Colon's Point. Colon Moore was supposed to head for the point of mangroves to his left of the inlet, but his dragline bucket struck a layer of coquina rock in deep water, and the dike was redirected. (Sanibel-Captiva Nature Calendar.)

When the dike was connected to the upland at each end, it created an 800-acre impoundment. The tide no longer flooded the flats inside the impoundment, but rainfall flooded it because there was no way to discharge surplus water. Plans called for installation of a series of water-control structures to permit interchange between the impoundment, but the first attempt was inadequate. In this 1966 photograph, part-time maintenance worker Bob Sabatino inspects a rainfall-caused washout that damaged a section of original culvert. (USFWS.)

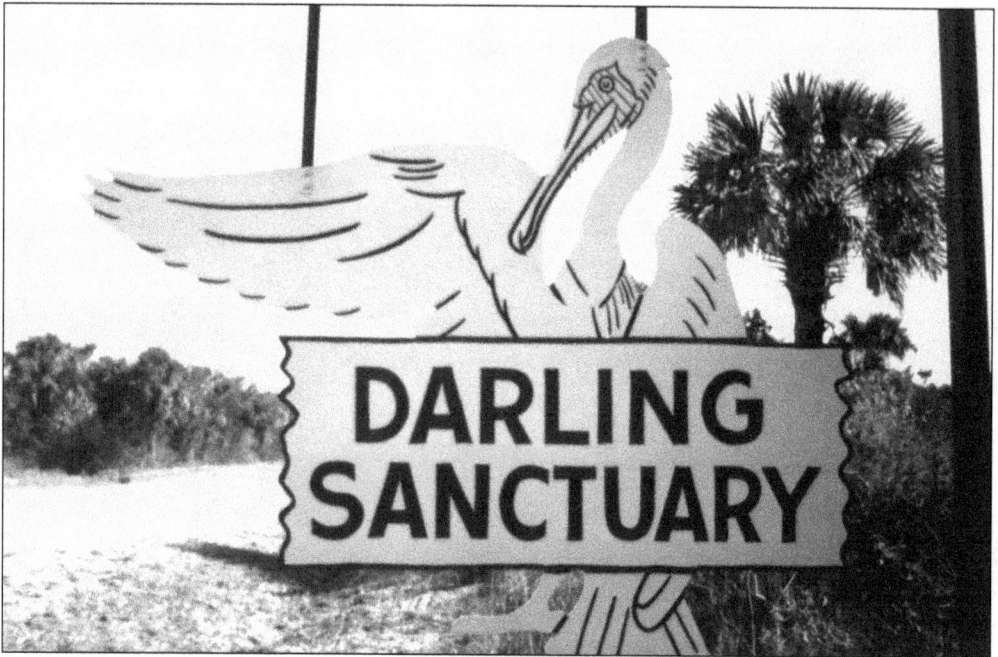

Some people use the term *sanctuary* to identify the refuge. It is neither a sanctuary, nor a reserve, nor a preserve, nor a park. It is a National Wildlife Refuge. The J.N. "Ding" Darling Memorial Sanctuary Committee (JNDDMSC) erected the above directional sign in 1965, before the Service authorized the installation of an official sign. This sign was located on Sanibel-Captiva Road and pointed across the highway to the entrance of the new dike and later Wildlife Drive. The photograph below is from 1967. This is the first official sign erected at the entrance to Wildlife Drive. It was manufactured to Service standards and paid for by the Sanibel-Captiva Conservation Foundation (SCCF). The JNDDMSC had evolved into the SCCF in 1967, and they agreed to drop the word *sanctuary* altogether in 1969, when the Service advised them it incorrectly identified the refuge and was unacceptable. (Above, author; below, USFWS.)

Over 250 species of birds have been recorded on the refuge, or other parts of the islands. Serious bird watchers (known as birders) tout Sanibel as a must-visit destination. Birders were astounded in 1972 when a pair of American flamingos (pictured above) took up residence in the refuge's west impoundment. A few weeks later, they disappeared as quietly as they had made their appearance, and their origins were never determined. The birds may have been escapees or wanderers from a small wild flock that shows up in southern Florida periodically. The photograph below, taken during an extreme low tide in 1989, demonstrates the density of water birds that use the refuge's tidal flats for foraging. For optimum bird-watching opportunities, it is best to visit at low tide, because thousands of egrets, herons, ibises, and shorebirds often congregate for an avian feeding frenzy. (Above, author; below, Sanibel-Captiva Nature Calendar.)

A species of South Florida snake has adapted over time and is able to cope with and live in the tidal ecosystem's saltwater habitat. The harmless mangrove salt marsh snake, pictured above, frequents the mangrove forest. It comes in two major color variations, helping it conceal itself perfectly in the prop root system of the red mangroves. Colors of this small, two-foot-long, fish-eating snake range from gray to red. Only two of southern Florida's four venomous snakes have been recorded on Sanibel and the refuge: the eastern coral snake and the eastern diamondback rattlesnake (pictured below). Once, both were considered common snakes on Sanibel, but the coral snake is now categorized as rare, and the diamondback rattlesnake is possibly extirpated on the island. This small specimen was photographed on a shell ridge in the refuge in 1988. Neither the dusky pigmy rattlesnake nor the cottonmouth, both also venomous, have been recorded on Sanibel at this writing. (Above, Sanibel-Captiva Nature Calendar; below, author.)

When water birds congregate on the exposed mud flats along Wildlife Drive, taking advantage of accessible prey resources at low tide, people congregate, too. This is exemplified in the picture, as serious photographers line up trying to capture the perfect shot with an array of expensive long lenses. Over time, the birds have become accustomed to the close approach of people. This results in some exceptional photographs. (USFWS.)

Early on, the Sanibel-Captiva Conservation Foundation funded public use projects on the refuge with grants they received from the Alice O'Brien Foundation. O'Brien was a close friend and neighbor of the Darlings when they wintered on Captiva. The design for this pointing pelican was adapted from one of "Ding" Darling's creations. A series of these signs served as markers for a five-mile canoe trail that meandered through the red mangrove forest from McIntyre Creek to Colon's Point. (Author.)

The Alice O'Brien Foundation channeled funds to the Sanibel-Captiva Conservation Foundation for additional public-use purposes on the refuge. The Alice O'Brien Tower, pictured here, was a duplicate of the wooden Bailey Tract Bird Tower. The structure was funded and built in 1966. It was replaced in 2002 with a modern concrete and steel structure. (USFWS.)

In 1967, the Sanibel-Captiva Conservation Foundation also funded construction of this Red Mangrove Overlook, accessible from Wildlife Drive. The wire was installed to prevent would-be shell collectors from reaching the mudflats. The visitors are unidentified. (USFWS.)

In 1976, the Service contracted to construct a cross dike to connect the Wildlife Drive with the Indigo Trail. This divided the impoundment into separate east and west impoundments. The cross dike is in the center of this 1980 photograph. The water in the west impoundment became extremely fresh by 1977 because of heavier-than-usual rainfall. Without any overflow, the salinity in the impoundment was reduced, and it soon supported large populations of frogs and freshwater fishes. The west impoundment became known among islanders as the freshwater side. (Sanibel-Captiva Nature Calendar.)

# J.N. "DING" DARLING NWR

## J.N. "Ding" Darling
### National Wildlife Refuge

The above map illustrates the points of interest and available visitor amenities in the units of J.N. "Ding" Darling National Wildlife Refuge on Sanibel and nearby Buck Key. Sanibel's main roads are identified, and refuge lands administered by the Service are shaded. In 1979, work started on the installation of seven permanent water-control structures on Wildlife Drive. The flashboard gates of these huge culverts were set at a fixed elevation in an attempt to retain an optimal level of water inside the impoundments, while allowing any surplus water to overflow into the estuary. For half of the year, the gates were open to permit regular tidal interchange. When the gates were closed, a very large population of blue crabs congregated just inside the structures. In the photograph below from 1995, Amber Young Weeks helps to net part of a delicious blue crab dinner. (Above, USFWS; below, Leslie LeBuff Young.)

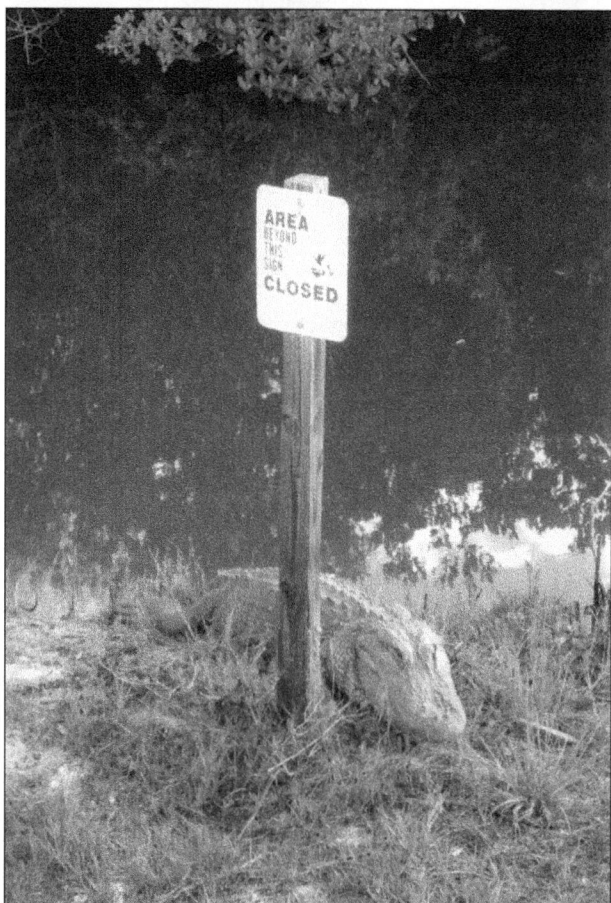

The seven permanent water-control structures, one of which is pictured above, gave the refuge a tool to better manage the impoundments. Is it not said, "A picture is worth a thousand words?" With its brief message, the closed-area sign in the photograph at left exemplifies the meaning of the above statement. This unique photograph demands the attention of the viewer by its very composition, and demonstrates that signs on national wildlife refuges mean something. The basking alligator is certainly proving that point. (Above, USFWS; left, Janice Howland Rubinski.)

The tidal bayous and creeks of the refuge have always been productive for sport and commercial fishermen, until Florida's constitution was amended in 1994 by a voter-approved referendum, which stopped commercial gill-net fishing in the state. Until then, striped mullet were the most targeted commercial species in Sanibel waters. Snook are the primary game fish in the mangrove system. Chuck LeBuff is pictured in 1995 with a 29-pound, 39-inch snook he took on live shrimp, in one of his favorite deep holes on the refuge, located in McIntyre Creek. (Author.)

The surface of the main dike/Wildlife Drive disappeared into the atmosphere as dust, as the road was pulverized over time by vehicles. The drive also became treacherously soft in spots and required unpopular closures. Shell-based resurfacing by contractors helped, but resulted in a much dustier surface. This posed health and safety issues for exposed hikers and bicyclists. In 2001, the drive was paved with a semi-permeable rock surface. Paving and other improvements, which included larger replacement water-control structures, reached a cost of $1.4 million. The refuge's resident American crocodile high-steps as she tests the feel of the new pavement. (USFWS.)

# Six

# LAND ACQUISITION AND BOUNDARY EXPANSION

At the time of the refuge's creation in 1945, it was administered by Daniel B. Beard (1906–1977), manager of the Everglades National Wildlife Refuge, headquartered in Dania, Florida. Beard transferred to the National Park Service to become the first superintendent of Everglades National Park in 1947. The Sanibel NWR then became part of a complex known as South Florida NWRs, managed by Gerald F. Baker (1902–1963). Five years later, the headquarters was relocated to Loxahatchee NWR, near Boynton Beach. Sanibel NWR remained part of this complex, until 1971. Project leaders who succeeded Baker and supervised Sanibel NWR operations include, in order of service, Frederick A. Cunningham (1909–1989), Jacob M. Valentine (1917–2000), William H. Julian (1926–), Richard L. Thompson (1935–), and John R. Eadie (1937–). In 1971, the J.N. "Ding" Darling NWR became a stand-alone station, managed by Bob Barber, and was directly supervised by staff in the Atlanta Regional Office.

In the beginning, the Fish and Wildlife Service was not the largest landowner on Sanibel. By 1954, the agency owned the 100-acre Bailey Tract, leased the 50-acre Coast Guard parcel on Point Ybel, and leased 2,392 acres of mostly tidal mangrove forest on the northern part of Sanibel from the State of Florida. In the early 1960s, the 3.2-acre beachfront Perry Tract was added, a gift to the refuge from the estate of Dr. Louise Perry. After prompting by island conservation groups, the Service made a commitment to bring as much land as possible inside an approved boundary that was designated in 1967.

A Concept Plan for land acquisition and development on Sanibel was published by the Service that year. The acquisition of privately owned parcels was a slow and expensive proposition, but most were acquired after purchases were negotiated between the Service and willing sellers. Several large tracts that appeared destined for real estate development were owned by unwilling sellers. One of these subdivisions fronted on Tarpon Bay, and the developer was already selling lots. This vital tract was acquired after a Declaration of Taking was issued and condemnation of the land proceeded through the federal court system. J.N. "Ding" Darling NWR now contains over 6,400 acres owned, leased, or otherwise administered by the Fish and Wildlife Service. "Ding" Darling would be pleased.

# J. N. "Ding" Darling
## National Wildlife Refuge

Lee County, Florida

This Concept Plan was published in August 1967. The title page states: "A PROSPECTUS. This Concept Plan embodies a concise presentation of objectives, broad management guidelines, and development proposals sufficient to assure a systematic operation of the J.N. "Ding" Darling National Wildlife Refuge, both as a sanctuary for wildlife and as an area for public enjoyment of the fish and wildlife and natural resources." (USFWS.)

# J.N. "DING" DARLING NATIONAL WILDLIFE REFUGE
## WILDERNESS STUDY AREA

### LEE COUNTY, FLORIDA

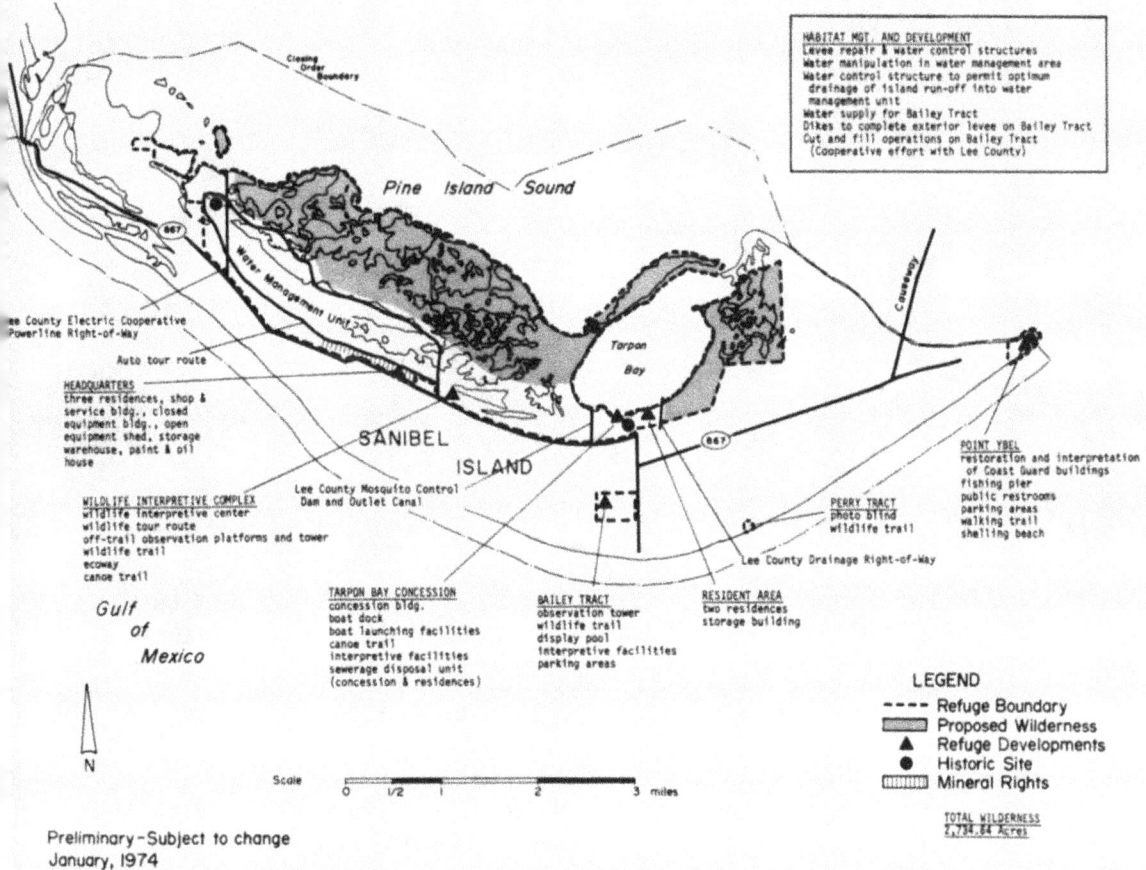

HABITAT MGT. AND DEVELOPMENT
Levee repair & water control structures
Water manipulation in water management area
Water control structure to permit optimum
drainage of island run-off into water
management unit
Water supply for Bailey Tract
Dikes to complete exterior levee on Bailey Tract
Cut and fill operations on Bailey Tract
(Cooperative effort with Lee County)

Pine  Island  Sound

ee County Electric Cooperative
Powerline Right-of-Way

Auto tour route

Tarpon
Bay

HEADQUARTERS
three residences, shop &
service bldg., closed
equipment bldg., open
equipment shed, storage
warehouse, paint & oil
house

SANIBEL
ISLAND

POINT YBEL
restoration and interpretation
of Coast Guard buildings
fishing pier
public restrooms
parking areas
walking trail
shelling beach

Lee County Mosquito Control
Dam and Outlet Canal

WILDLIFE INTERPRETIVE COMPLEX
wildlife interpretive center
wildlife tour route
off-trail observation platforms and tower
wildlife trail
ecoway
canoe trail

PERRY TRACT
photo blind
wildlife trail

Lee County Drainage Right-of-Way

Gulf
of
Mexico

TARPON BAY CONCESSION
concession bldg.
boat dock
boat launching facilities
canoe trail
interpretive facilities
sewerage disposal unit
(concession & residences)

BAILEY TRACT
observation tower
wildlife trail
display pool
interpretive facilities
parking areas

RESIDENT AREA
two residences
storage building

### LEGEND

- - - - Refuge Boundary
▨▨▨ Proposed Wilderness
▲ Refuge Developments
● Historic Site
▥▥▥ Mineral Rights

TOTAL WILDERNESS
2,734.84 Acres

N

Scale
0   1/2   1   2   3 miles

Preliminary – Subject to change
January, 1974

The National Wilderness Preservation System was created in 1964 when Pres. Lyndon Johnson signed the National Wilderness Act. No matter their size, any roadless island already owned as part of a NWR was eligible to be included in this system. In 1976, most of the mangrove forest of J.N. "Ding" Darling National Wildlife Refuge—2,619 acres situated north of Wildlife Drive—and the islands of small satellite refuge Island Bay NWR became national wilderness areas. (USFWS.)

After procrastinating because he did not approve of naming refuges after people, secretary of the interior Stewart Udall finally signed the authorization that renamed the Sanibel NWR to J.N. "Ding" Darling NWR, on August 15, 1967. The expensive land acquisition program was essentially completed in January 1973. The renaming was not formally celebrated until February 4, 1978. In the photograph taken during that celebration, a crowd of islanders and distinguished guests have gathered at the Alice O'Brien Tower on the refuge's Wildlife Drive for the official renaming ceremony. Dignitaries on the platform are, from left to right, Lawrence Givens, regional refuge supervisor; Robert Brantly, director, Florida Game and Fresh Water Fish Commission; Sherry Fisher, president, J.N. "Ding" Darling Foundation; Emmy Lu Lewis, chairman, Sanibel-Captiva Conservation Foundation; Robert Herbst, assistant secretary of the interior; and Lynn Greenwalt, director, Fish and Wildlife Service. (USFWS.)

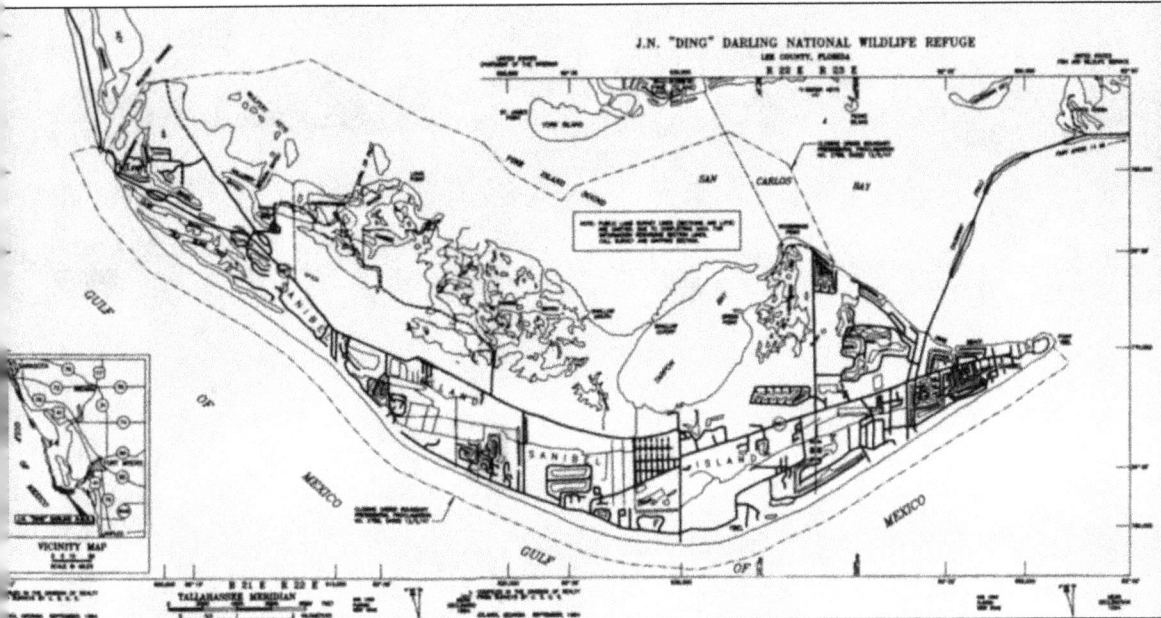

This is a boundary map of J.N. "Ding" Darling NWR from 1996. When the Fish and Wildlife Service committed to a land acquisition program on Sanibel in 1967, the agency pulled out all the stops. The state-owned acreage that was originally leased for refuge purposes was transferred to the Service in exchange for Anclote Key NWR and another tract of public land in North Florida. This transfer included ownership of not only mangrove-forested tidal lands, but also the open bay bottoms. (USFWS.)

The refuge became part of the national Recreation Fee Program on December 1, 1987. In the beginning, this operated under the honor system, but over time, the program evolved to have an entrance booth on Wildlife Drive where the entrance fee is collected. In this photograph, refuge staffer Linda Brown offers visitors directions and basic information about the refuge from her booth at the base of the entrance ramp leading up to the Visitor Center. Initially, the cost of entry to Wildlife Drive was three dollars per vehicle unless someone in the vehicle was in possession of a valid Duck Stamp or another Federal Land Passport. These were sold in the Visitor Center and allow free entry. (USFWS.)

# Seven

# COMMUNITY INVOLVEMENT

Refuge managers Wood and Barber meshed their personal lives with the people and organizations of the island communities. Both men did so with skilled diplomacy, and this forte of good will was continued until the Service's chain of command changed. In 1977, the Fish and Wildlife Service reorganized, adding a layer of supervision between the regional offices and the field stations. The regions were subdivided into areas, each overseen by an area manager. Donald Hankla (1927–2007) managed the Jacksonville Area Office and supervised refuges in Florida, Georgia, the US Virgin Islands, and Puerto Rico. For the next four years, the special connection that had been forged between the island's residents and the Service, through the diplomacy of managers Wood and Barber, began to unravel. The first three refuge managers had the full support of regional director Walter Gresh and regional refuge supervisor Lawrence Givens. Bill Ashe, of the Division of Realty, worked tirelessly in the land acquisition efforts. These visionaries supported the people of Sanibel-Captiva and cleared the pathway to help islanders develop a fitting memorial to "Ding" Darling. That direct one-on-one connection to the Regional Office was eliminated, and for the next few years, refuge management did not integrate well into the island community. The area manager ascended to office after the retirement of Gresh and Givens and was, therefore, totally unfamiliar with the history—the base of extremely close cooperation between the Service and the island communities that had been nurtured over the years. During Hankla's rein, he took a hard line on issues of interest to the islands. He relied on national policies of the Service and wanted those rules applied toward refuge management locally. It was with his attitude that the special dispensation for the islands would end. A series of management decisions sent signals that frustrated a few islanders, mostly retirees and a few who once held auspicious positions in government or were notable scientists. Some grew publicly hostile against the management style of the refuge between 1974 and 1983.

The area offices were eliminated in 1981, and by 1984, after Refuge Manager Albert R. "Ron" Hight came on board, the cooperative interaction between the refuge and the island community trended toward restoration.

From the beginning, the refuge supported the all-volunteer fire abatement force on Sanibel. The Sanibel Fire Control District was officially created by the Florida State Legislature in 1955. In this photograph from about 1956, the volunteers are pictured with their fire truck. From left to right are (first row) Jack Cole, Chief Martin Hiers, refuge manager Tommy Wood, John Peurifoy, Glen Rhodes, Bill Way, Jimmy Jack, and Bill Reisinger; (second row), Charles "Chuck" Nave, Francis Bailey, Vince McVettie, James "Doc" Pickens, Jake Stokes, Charles M. Rhodes, Charles E. "Pop" Rhodes, Clarence Rutland, and an unidentified person. (Raymond Rhodes.)

Boy Scouts of America Sanibel-Captiva Troop 88 is pictured in 1969. Assisting in a local Boy Scout troop was important to refuge manager Tommy Wood, and he encouraged Charles LeBuff to become a scoutmaster and form this troop. From left to right are (first row) Marshall Tilton, Gary Holtzman (deceased), Ronnie Gavin, Kim Billheimer, Mark Muench (deceased), Lee Woodring, and Charlie Gavin; (second row) Paul Zajicek, David Zajicek, John Cimato, J.R. Broadbent, Harry Jordan, Hans Wilson, and Wayne Woodring. (Author.)

Below, Sanibel Boy Scout David Zajicek holds a brown pelican nestling and Charles LeBuff bands the bird on Upper Bird Key, part of Matlacha Pass NWR. This is one of several small, but important, colonial bird rookeries in Matlacha Pass NWR. This island produces an average of 400 brown pelicans each year. This refuge, originally three islands, was established in 1908 by Pres. Theodore Roosevelt. Today, it contains 28 islands. In the 1970s, J.N. "Ding" Darling NWR cooperated with the Louisiana Department of Wildlife and Fisheries and permitted that agency to collect a number of young brown pelicans from Pine Island and Pinellas NWRs to restock pelicans in Louisiana. After all, the brown pelican is the state bird of Louisiana, and the species was almost extirpated there. The caged birds in the photograph above were transported to Louisiana. The men are unidentified. (Above, USFWS; below, Edward Phillips.)

When the refuge had a small staff and all resided on the islands, they were involved in most aspects of island life. Staff members were in demand as speakers for civic and conservation organizations, and served on island-based committees. In the photograph at left from 1961, Charles LeBuff is speaking to a Girl Scout leaders group about local snakes. In the photograph below, from 1973, LeBuff (wearing the Service's dress uniform) discusses a box turtle shell while making one of his weekly wildlife presentations to a class at Sanibel Elementary School. (Both, USFWS.)

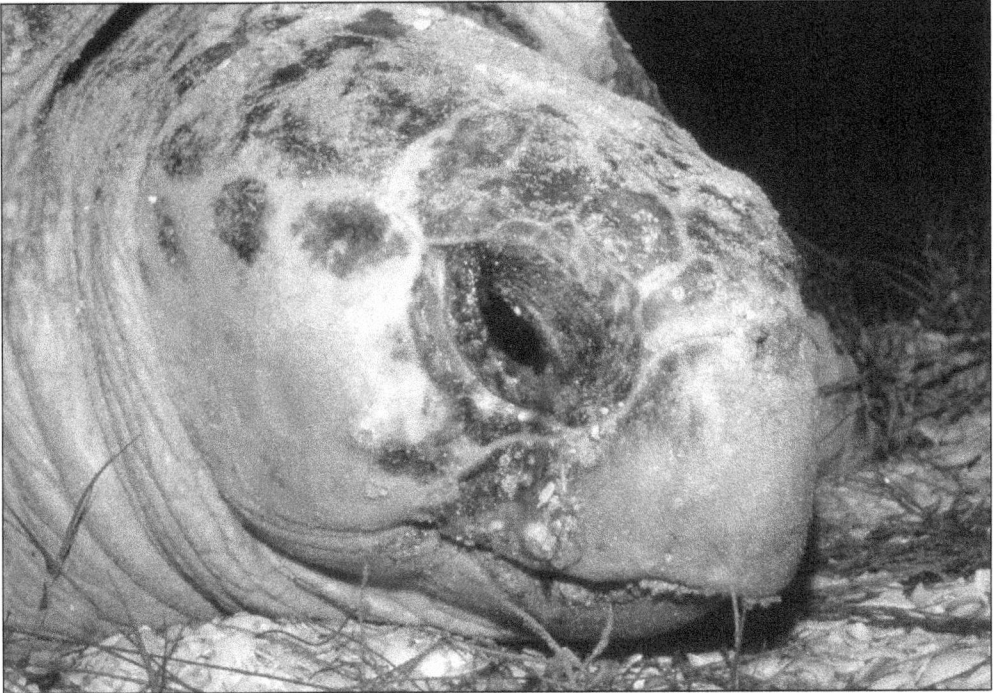

The quasi-official refuge sea turtle conservation program was suggested to Charles LeBuff by "Ding" Darling. This was fully supported by refuge manager Wood and implemented in May 1960. Refuge staff members were authorized to enforce federal regulations. They were also commissioned deputy Florida wildlife officers, which enabled them to enforce state wildlife-related statutes. Refuge manager Wood had patrolled the Sanibel beach since 1949 to protect nesting loggerhead turtles, pictured above. The photograph below was taken by assistant manager Patrick D. Hagan. He submitted this photograph of a post-nesting island loggerhead turtle and won the Service's 1976 employee photograph contest, in the endangered species category. (Above, author; below, Caretta Research, Inc.)

Refuge staff implemented studies to determine if there were techniques that could be applied to protect in situ loggerhead turtle eggs. An excessive population of raccoons also patrolled the beaches and consumed all sea turtle eggs that they found. Charles LeBuff began to tag loggerheads on Sanibel in 1964, as shown in the above photograph. The tagging program was continued until 1991. The photograph below shows loggerhead turtle eggs being deposited on the Sanibel beach in 1969. Female loggerheads nest every two years, and they lay multiple nests about every 12 nights. In 1973, one tagged Sanibel loggerhead repeatedly returned, depositing a total of 920 eggs during six observed nestings that summer. A clutch averages about 110 soft-shelled, Ping Pong ball–size eggs. The hatchlings emerge from the sand in approximately 55 days. (Above, Warren Boutchia; below, author.)

This 1970 photograph, taken from the porch of Lighthouse Quarters 2, shows the loggerhead turtle hatchery at refuge headquarters. Beginning in 1969, jeopardized eggs were moved into this compound from other parts of the 12-mile Sanibel beach to prevent their consumption by raccoons. During some summers, these predators would eat up to 90 percent of the loggerhead eggs produced. Up to 5,500 eggs were buried in this hatchery each summer until it was deactivated later in the decade. (Author.)

Loggerhead hatchlings are heaped up on the seaward side of their retainer in 1970. Emerging from the sand, usually at night in natural situations, the turtles orient to the brightest source of light, which in the best of circumstances is the seaward horizon. For two years, hatchlings were placed in saltwater tanks at a sea turtle farm, which was operated by Caretta Research as a head-start facility and located next to the privately owned Tarpon Bay Marina. (Author.)

101

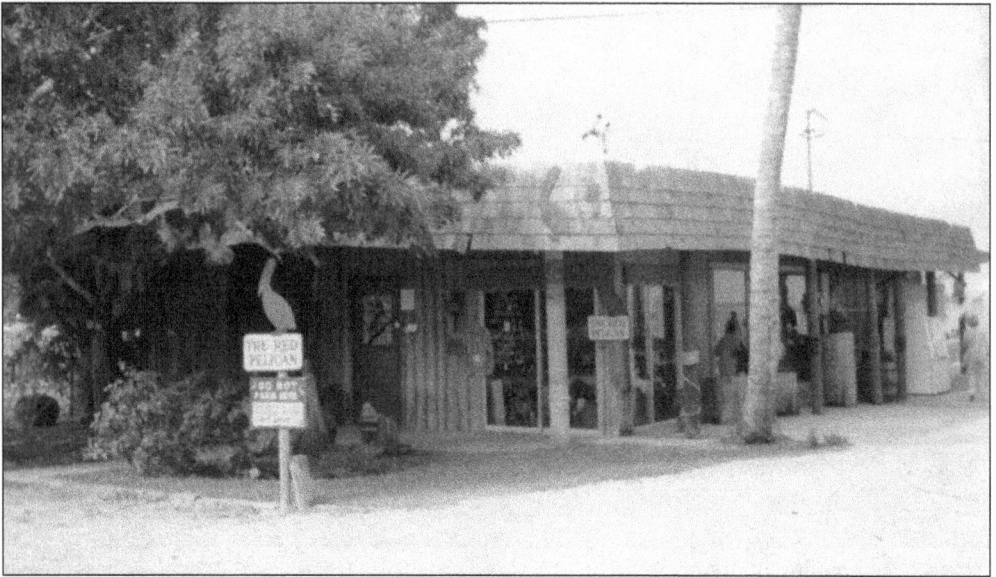

The former Red Pelican Gift Shop at Tarpon Bay Marina was photographed in about 1967. This parcel, originally the Casa Ybel Marina, was purchased by the Service in 1972, and this gift shop was demolished. Today, a building located west of the former Red Pelican site houses Tarpon Bay Explorers, the refuge concession operation. The sea turtle farm was situated about 200 feet to the east of this gift shop. In the photograph below, Charles and Jean LeBuff are enjoying the self-guided Commodore Creek canoe trail. This waterway is accessible from the refuge's concession operation on Tarpon Bay. This meandering, tunnel-like stream and its connected tidal lakes make up an excellent example of a wild mangrove creek ecosystem. This waterway is one of the most popular recreational sites on the refuge and continues to attract many visitors into the interesting realm of a nearly impenetrable and ecologically important red mangrove forest. (Above, Deb McQuade Gleason; below, Gerri Much.)

These photographs from 1969 are of Caretta Research's sea turtle farm on the shore of Tarpon Bay. This compound contained compartmentalized tanks to house sibling groups of loggerhead turtle hatchlings. The turtles were fed a combination of commercially available food and ground fish. The plan was to rear them to a large enough size in captivity so they could better cope with predators at sea. Water was pumped from the bay, but problems arose when winter temperatures adversely affected the little turtles. This curtailed the head-starting effort, and this part of Caretta Research's program was eliminated. The photograph below shows the inside of the brand-new facility, which had all good intentions but was ultimately unsuccessful. Floating tanks were later installed for limited sea turtle rehabilitation at the dock of the nearby refuge housing area in cooperation with the refuge. (Both, author.)

The first contingent of little loggerheads raised at Tarpon Bay was released in May 1970, in a public event at the Sanibel Lighthouse. Islanders turned out for this release, and children from the community were enlisted to turn the 10-month-old turtles loose. In this photograph, a flotilla of turtles has just been released by the excited young people, and they are ready to launch another. (Author.)

Beginning in 1977, the refuge cooperated with the National Sea Turtle Stranding and Salvage Network. Dead marine turtles, assumed to have been drowned offshore in shrimp nets, frequently strand on the Captiva and Sanibel beaches. In this 1985 photograph, a dead loggerhead turtle is being measured. The remains were picked up on the beach by the City of Sanibel and hauled to a disposal site on the refuge. The few live turtles that stranded and were judged to have survival potential were moved to the Clearwater Marine Science Center for rehabilitation. The others were euthanized. (Edward Phillips.)

When the Lee County Commission proposed a plan to allow 90,000 people to live on Sanibel, island residents incorporated to control their density—and destiny. Refuge manager Bob Barber was active in the pre-incorporation Sanibel-Captiva Planning Committee as islanders searched for ways to manage development. Charles LeBuff served the community for six years as a two-term councilman. Although a federal employee, he could participate because the election was nonpartisan. The first council, seated in 1974, is identified from left to right as follows: (first row) Zelda Butler (1926–1981) and Francis Bailey (1921–); (second row) Porter Goss (1938–), Vernon MacKenzie (1906–1982), and Charles LeBuff (1936–). Goss went on to become a US Congressman and director of the Central Intelligence Agency. (City of Sanibel.)

Refuge manager Delano "Del" Pierce, along with his wife, Norma, and their two children, transferred from Kootenai NWR in northern Idaho to become manager of J.N. "Ding" Darling NWR on November 21, 1977. In the above staff photograph from 1979 are, from left to right, (first row) Ferrell Johns, Del Pierce, and Larry Narcisse; (second row) Donna Stanek, Edythe Stokes, Dolores Ambrose, Charles LeBuff, and Nicola "Nick" Tirelli (1930–2009). In the photograph below from 1981 are, from left to right, manager Del Pierce, assistant manager Larry Narcisse, outdoor recreation planner Donna Stanek, assistant manager of Tampa Bay NWRs Bill Black, and biological technician Charles LeBuff. (Both, USFWS.)

# *Eight*

# PARTNERSHIPS

Interagency partnerships and cooperative agreements worked well for those who managed the J.N. "Ding" Darling National Wildlife Refuge. The most significant of these was between the refuge and Lee County Mosquito Control District. From the time the district launched mosquito control and water management operations on Sanibel, refuge manager Tommy Wood and district director T. Wayne Miller worked cooperatively until Wood's retirement. The district's ditching program in the Sanibel Slough was successful, in terms of both mosquito abatement and bringing elusive permanent fresh surface water to Sanibel. At manager Wood's request, the district expeditiously excavated the Seaplane Canal along the southern boundary of the Bailey Tract for use as a base for the refuge aircraft. Tommy moved the seaplane from Tarpon Bay to its new home on November 16, 1959. No longer would the floatplane be regularly exposed to corrosive saltwater.

On October 2, 1962, the draglines moved north of Sanibel-Captiva Road and started building a mosquito-control dike that would be four miles long at completion. This dike followed an unsurveyed route and meandered through the red mangrove forest. The chief dragline operator, Colon Moore, and manager Wood made weekly flights in the seaplane to select the next point of mangroves that Colon should aim for. This dike became controversial a few years later. One county conservation group threatened a lawsuit and wanted it removed, claiming this dike had a negative impact on the local estuary because there was no interchange between the impounded and tidal waters. But, had Wood and Miller not worked together, the dike's development as a tool to reduce mosquito populations and to coincidentally create the popular Wildlife Drive, would not have happened. The dike was built at no cost to the federal government. In the 1990s, other partnerships developed, and manager Louis Hinds brought this concept to a new level. Under his purview, the refuge partnered with the City of Sanibel, the Sanibel-Captiva Conservation Foundation, the "Ding" Darling Wildlife Society, Lee County Electric Cooperative, and the Lee County School Board. These functional partnerships were forged with habitat improvement and the mission of the refuge as the paramount driving force.

The permanent staff in the above photograph from 1986 are, from left to right, (first row) Dolores Ambrose, Richard Blackburn, Ralph Lloyd, Ferrell Johns, and Edythe Stokes; (second row) Kristie Seaman Anders, Charles LeBuff, manager Ron Hight, and Chris Olsen Zajicek. The staff soared to 19 employees by late 1991. Pictured in the photograph below are, from left to right,: (first row) Ralph Lloyd, Richard Blackburn, Edythe Stokes, Virginia Saunders, Ferrell Johns, and Nancy Haugen; (second row) Herb Dulberg, manager Lou Hinds, Randy Druckman, Bill Varga, and Randy Cordray. (Both, USFWS.)

Selected employees were delegated federal law enforcement authority by the Migratory Bird Treaty Act of 1918, later expanded after passage of the Endangered Species Act. Refuge officers wore badges, carried firearms, and had arrest powers, but were not uniformed until 1961. Law enforcement authority was considered collateral duty. Beginning in 1978, each officer was required to attend the Federal Law Enforcement Training Center in Glynco, Georgia. Pictured next to the refuge's Aquasport patrol boat are, from left to right, assistant refuge manager Ralph Lloyd, refuge manager Ron Hight, biological technician Charles LeBuff, and outdoor recreation planner Chris Olsen Zajicek (1952–2002). In the photograph below, Charles LeBuff and his wife, Jean, are target shooting at the Lee County Sheriff's Department firing range, shortly before Charles traveled to the Florida Law Enforcement Training Center in Quincy, Florida, for required annual firearms requalification. (Both, USFWS.)

Temporary refuge employees Frank Ligas and Edmund Gavin Jr. hand-pulled cattails in Stewart Pond in the mid-1950s. In 1958, the refuge excavated two impounded pools and drilled two six-inch artesian wells in the Bailey Tract. These pools proved too shallow, and cattails invaded and soon choked them. This did not improve the wintering waterfowl habitat the project was designed to enhance. By 1965, the herbicide Dalapon became the standard way to fight cattails. A crawler tractor was used to pull a spray rig through the marsh to apply the chemical. In the above photograph from 1968, a crew from the Lee County Mosquito Control District is mixing the water-based herbicide preparatory to loading the mix in their helicopter's spray tanks. In the photograph below, the helicopter is applying Dalapon over the cattail-infested wetlands. (Both, USFWS.)

By 1977, the long, close partnership between the refuge and the Lee County Mosquito Control District (LCMCD) began to wane. Sanibel resident environmentalist George Campbell (1918–2004) raised issues about the chemicals the district was applying in their aerial adulticiding and larviciding activities on Sanibel and Captiva. Baytex was used to control adult mosquitoes, and Abate was used for the larvae. Campbell argued the district was applying these pesticides contrary to their labels and the rules of the US Environmental Protection Agency. By 1990, the refuge shifted position, relative to previously approved chemical applications on their lands by the district, and demanded changes in the mosquito control program. Mosquito control on Sanibel became more difficult, and by 1994 the larvicide Abate could no longer be applied at the former strength on refuge lands. In the photograph, the skilled pilots of three ancient DC-3s, part of the LCMCD's still-flying air fleet, are applying Baytex at dawn above western Sanibel in 1972. (Lee County Mosquito Control District.)

By 1967, Captiva Road was tumbling into the Gulf of Mexico because of beach erosion. Lee County needed an on-island spoil site to reduce the costs of hauling fill from the mainland to repair the road. They approached the refuge, and a cooperative agreement was signed, permitting the county to dig and stockpile thousands of cubic yards of fill dirt on the Bailey Tract for county road purposes. In the photograph, the fill has stabilized Captiva Road, which has been armored with stone riprap. (Captiva Erosion Prevention District.)

Quantities of fill were required to raise elevations at the construction sites of the maintenance center and administrative building. These are located on either side of the school on Sanibel-Captiva Road. The site preparation contractor for the new refuge facilities was allowed to obtain fill by creating additional pools in the Bailey Tract, as pictured. (USFWS.)

112

Fire is always a threat whenever the Sanibel Slough is at its driest. The Sanibel Fire Control District customarily responded and extinguished blazes for the public safety and welfare, without considering how important fire is to the healthy ecology of the slough. It was not until most of the land was owned by conservation entities that prescribed fire became a routine management tool. In the photograph, refuge staff is conducting a large controlled burn along Sanibel-Captiva Road. (Paul Ryan, USFWS.)

The permanent staff assigned to the refuge is pictured in 1995. From left to right are, (first row) Manager Lou Hinds; (second row) Carol Pratt and Steve Alvarez; (third row) Edythe Stokes and Carroll Branyon; (fourth row) Linda Patton, Scott Player, and Layne Hamilton; (fifth row) Ferrell Johns, Julie Hiller, and Richard Blackburn. (USFWS.)

On the morning of May 9, 1980, refuge manager Del Pierce and Tampa Bay NWRs assistant manager Bill Black left the Coast Guard station on Egmont Key, where they had spent the night. They departed immediately after the station was notified of a disaster six miles to the east, in the center of Tampa Bay. A span of the Sunshine Skyway had collapsed when its supporting structure was struck by the freighter *Summit Venture*. The refuge boat raced to the site and was the second vessel on the scene. Del and Bill immediately began searching for survivors and found none, but they retrieved the body of one young victim, among the 35 people who perished in the tragedy that morning. The event was blamed on weather and operational failure of the on-board pilot who was in command of the ship. (USFWS.)

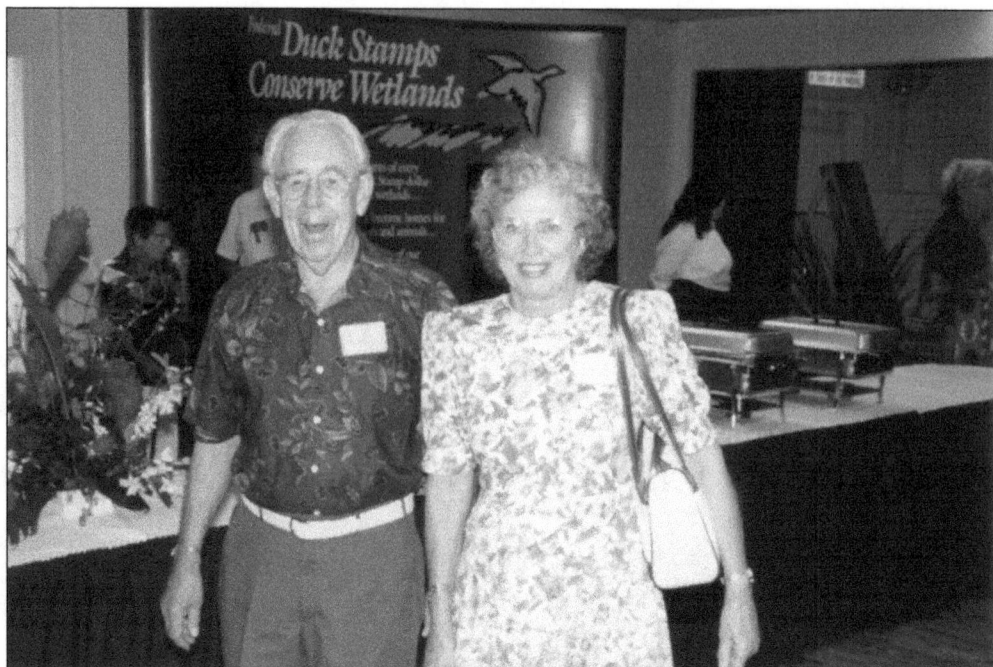

The "Ding" Darling Wildlife Society (DDWS), one of the first Refuge Friends groups in the nation, was formed in 1982 as a cooperative effort between refuge staff and private individuals who had an interest in the Service's local mission and wanted to provide support to the refuge. In the above photograph are first president of the DDWS, Burwell "Bud" Ryckman, and his wife, Martha. They are celebrating the refuge's 50th birthday in 1995. The photograph below was taken inside the Education Center, built in 1999, for which the DDWS raised $3.3 million, entirely from the private sector. Recently, 265 volunteers donated over 27,000 hours, assisting with interpretive programs at schools and the refuge, staffing the Education Center, and serving as naturalist rovers on Wildlife Drive. (Both, USFWS.)

In the photograph at right, Willard Scott, part-time Sanibel resident and NBC-TV personality, gives the keynote speech at the refuge's 50th birthday party in 1995. Hurricane Charley, a powerful, Category 4 tropical cyclone, impacted Southwest Florida on Friday, August, 13, 2004. The eye of the storm, with surface winds reaching 150 miles per hour, is visible in the photograph below. Charley came ashore 10 miles north of the refuge near Boca Grande Pass. This was the first direct hit by a major hurricane on Lee County's barrier islands since Hurricane Donna walloped them on September 10, 1960. (Right, USFWS; below, National Oceanic and Atmospheric Administration.)

Sanibel and Captiva roads were impassable for several days following the ferocity of Hurricane Charley. With its concentrated central circulation, the hurricane moved forward at a good clip when it passed over the barrier islands. Had it been a slow-moving system, damage would have been more severe. Estimated property damage on Sanibel and Captiva Islands reached $1 billion. A cadre of governmental agencies and contractors arrived for the daunting task of cleanup and restoration of services. The above photograph shows the damaged, defoliated red mangroves near the exit of the refuge's Wildlife Drive. The photograph at left demonstrates how the towering Australian pines crisscrossed the main road of Sanibel after crashing to the ground. (Both, *Island Reporter.*)

In the above photograph, workers from many federal agencies have gathered at the refuge maintenance center to get their work-area assignments. Australian pine trees were planted for landscape purposes along Periwinkle Way and Captiva Road early in the 20th century. They were known to be weak, shallow-rooted, and vulnerable in hurricane force winds. In the photograph below, young Zachary Farst is inspecting the root system of an 85-year-old Australian pine that Hurricane Charley knocked over. (Above, Rob Jess, USFWS; below, *Island Reporter*.)

The refuge was a godsend in the storm's aftermath. Residents who evacuated were not allowed to return to their homes for five days after the hurricane. Roads were impassable because of fallen Australian pines, and there were no services. But refuge manager Rob Jess saved the day. He best describes the recovery himself: "We were able to umbrella the refuge support under the island's Incident Command System and bring 110 refuge employees, 23 pieces of heavy equipment, and some 45 chainsaw operators to the Island for recovery [in three weeks] . . . This 'idea' was devised by Lou [Hinds] and I, a few months before the hurricane ever hit . . . and it was sheer luck that our ideas came together and were on paper then tested by Hurricane Charley." In the photograph, a contingent from the Florida Division of Forestry is hard at work clearing Periwinkle Way. (*Island Reporter.*)

Heavy equipment, such as the loader in the photograph above, was dispersed throughout the islands. Skilled chainsaw operators bucked up the trees, loaders scooped out the complete root systems, and the trees were trucked to a centralized burn site that burned day and night. In a wise move by the city government, Australian pines that were still standing after the hurricane were removed from along the road network to eliminate impacts the tree species would have on recovery after future storms. The photograph at right captures a National Guard medical unit dispensing first aid to an injured worker. Surprisingly, despite the dangerous labor-intensive work and long hours, just a few human injuries were reported to officials. However, a Service firefighter was seriously injured in a tree-felling accident. (Both, *Island Reporter.*)

Few structures escaped the wrath of Charley's winds, not including this cottage at Captiva's 'Tween Waters Inn, shown here. Near the end of his life, "Ding" Darling spent his winters in this unit. An Australian pine crashed down on the building. Hundreds of islanders, who had smartly evacuated in advance of the hurricane, were not allowed to return to learn how their homes had fared until five days after the storm. Most residences on the islands suffered roof damage; however, some homes on Captiva, closer to the storm's center and more powerful winds, were totally destroyed. (*Island Reporter.*)

Sanibel's first refuge manager Tommy Wood, pictured at right in 1970, moved away after retiring in 1971. He lived out his remaining years at one of his most favorite places on earth, next to the sponge docks at Tarpon Springs. Tommy last visited Sanibel in 1978, and he died in February 1990 at age 87. His successor, Bob Barber, pictured below in 2009, retired from his regional office position in 1994. For several years thereafter, he and his wife, Julie, were associated with a missionary group and lived in Kenya. In early 1995, the third manager, Glen Bond (see page 67), ended his Service career at Santee National Wildlife Refuge, in South Carolina, where he and his wife, Jeannie, continue to live. (Right, USFWS; below, Robert Barber.)

Del Pierce (shown above in 1979) retired from Des Lacs NWR, North Dakota, in 1992. After retirement, Del and Norma Pierce returned to northern Idaho and built a home across the road from the house where Del was born. Ron Hight, pictured at left in October 1993, stayed at J.N. "Ding" Darling NWR until 1990, when he transferred to become manager of Merritt Island NWR, a position from which he retired in 2009. (Above, Del Pierce; left, Ron Hight.)

Lou Hinds (seen at right in 1995) transferred to Sanibel from the Service's central office in Washington, DC, in 1990. Lou was at J.N. "Ding" Darling NWR until 2001, when he accepted a supervisory position in the Atlanta Regional Office. Robert "Rob" Jess, pictured below in 2004, replaced Lou as refuge manager in 2001, transferring from the Atlanta Regional Office with his wife, Elisabeth, and their four sons. His Sanibel tenure included dealing with Hurricane Charley's aftermath in 2004. In this, his "finest hour," Rob Jess coordinated the Service's outstanding response to the disaster. In 2007, Rob was awarded the Citizen of the Year Award by the Sanibel-Captiva Chamber of Commerce. In 2008, he transferred to become manager of the Yukon Flats NWR, which is headquartered in Fairbanks, Alaska. (Right, *Island Reporter*; below, Rob Jess, USFWS.)

Pictured at left in 2011 is manager Paul Tritaik, who replaced Rob Jess. Tritaik transferred to Sanibel in 2008 with his wife, Rachel, and their son Liam, from Pelican Island and Archie Carr NWR. Edythe "Ede" Stokes (left) and author Charles LeBuff are pictured together in the photograph below, in 1990, just before LeBuff's retirement. Ede retired in 2000, after nearly 31 years of outstanding service at J.N. "Ding" Darling NWR. One of the author's wisest achievements was to recruit and hire Ede. After her untimely death in 2005, the refuge's administration building was named to honor her. (Both, USFWS.)

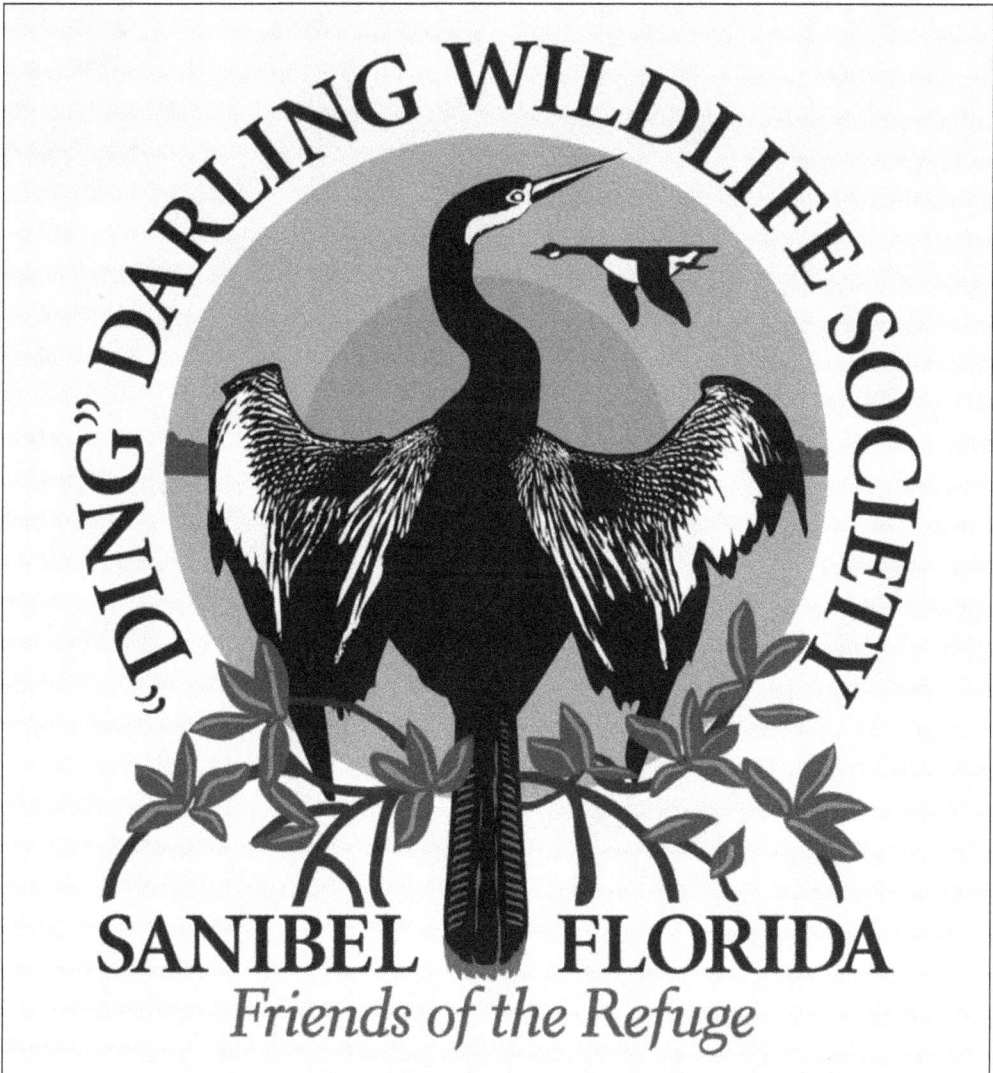

"DING" DARLING WILDLIFE SOCIETY

SANIBEL FLORIDA

*Friends of the Refuge*

With the creation in 1982 of the "Ding" Darling Wildlife Society-Friends of the Refuge (DDWS), the future of J.N "Ding" Darling National Wildlife Refuge took a dramatic turn toward accessibility. The society's formation came on the heels of the first visitor's center, when staff found themselves overwhelmed by visitors and in need of a volunteer program.

Since that day—through bookstore sales, philanthropic donations, and fundraising—DDWS has succeeded in building a newer $3.3 million Education Center, funding environmental education programs, supporting interns, and furthering public awareness for the more than 700,000 annual refuge visitors through publications and signage. The society also provides support for research equipment, school bus trips to the refuge, scholarships to budding environmentalists, and new and enhanced trails and boardwalks.

Government funding covers only a small portion of what it costs to manage a refuge the size and complexity of "Ding" Darling. As a result, the DDWS friends group helps with financial support when the federal budget falls short.

If you believe in the conservation and protection of our habitat and see the value of the J.N. "Ding" Darling National Wildlife Refuge, we hope you will become a Friend of the Refuge by joining the "Ding" Darling Wildlife Society. Please visit www.dingdarlingsociety.org today.

Visit us at
arcadiapublishing.com

www.ingramcontent.com/pod-product-compliance
Lightning Source LLC
Chambersburg PA
CBHW050639110426
42813CB00007B/1855